650 PATTERS
0003000044454
The gray fedora
Patterson, Kerry.
ATCHISON
2015-09-14

THE GRAY FEDORA

LESSONS ON LIFE, BUSINESS, AND EVERYTHING IN BETWEEN

By **KERRY PATTERSON**

New York Times bestselling author of
Crucial Conversations

Other *New York Times* bestselling books by
KERRY PATTERSON:

Crucial Conversations: Tools For Talking When Stakes are High

Crucial Accountability: Tools for Resolving Violated Expectations, Broken Commitments, and Bad Behavior

Influencer: The New Science of Leading Change

Change Anything: The New Science of Personal Success

PRAISE FOR THE GRAY FEDORA

"Heartwarming and profound lessons for all ages."

Shahid Khan, Innovation Evangelist & Mentor, Idea Curator, PayPal / eBay Inc.

"There are few writers who can capture the warmth and power of the human spirit like Kerry Patterson. Opening *The Gray Fedora* feels like you are being gathered around a campfire with your best friends, listening to their life stories, and experiencing their adventures. A shiver of sharks and professorial pig manure have never been so entertaining!"

Scot McCarthy, Director of Talent Development, CENTRA

"*The Gray Fedora* combines the wholesome wisdom of *Little House on the Prairie* meets The Waltons, with the business acumen and thought leadership of the *Harvard Business Review*. These short, poignant stories let us reflect on our strengths, weaknesses, passions, and especially our purpose. I would highly recommend reading a story or two whenever your soul needs soothing or your saw needs sharpening."

Pauline Lipkewich, Regional Vice President, LeadershipSmarts

"Kerry's eloquent delivery of these stories brings a range of reactions, from laughing out loud to heartfelt tenderness. Beyond the entertainment value of each story, each brings a lesson to learn or a reminder of past lessons learned."

Joseph Smith, Organization Development Specialist, Human Resources, UMass Memorial Health Care

"Kerry Patterson's wit is exceeded only by his wisdom. *The Gray Fedora* features stories from his life experiences; each vignette is woven into a poignant life lesson or profound business practice in this modern-day Aesop's Fables. You'll guffaw, you'll groan, and most importantly, you'll grow."

Mike Welsh, Learning & Development Consultant, Facebook

To
WILLIAM PATRICK NOONAN
The Man in the Gray Fedora

ISBN: 978-0-9961893-0-9 (Hardcover)
Library of Congress Control Number: 2015937150

Ordering Information:
Quantity sales. For information or to inquire about discounts on quantity purchases by corporations, associations, and others, contact the publisher at (800) 449-5989 or by email at editor@vitalsmarts.com.

Orders by U.S. trade bookstores and wholesalers. Please contact the publisher at (800) 449-5989 or by email at editor@vitalsmarts.com.

First Edition

CONTENTS

BUSINESS LESSONS

HOLIDAY LESSONS

CONCLUSION

A CALL TO WORDS

//

"There are a thousand thoughts lying within a man that
he does not know till he takes up a pen to write."

WILLIAM THACKERAY

One evening when my neighbor, Dr. Allen Christenson (a professor of Mayan language and culture), was compiling a dictionary of the Mayan language in the wilds of Guatemala, he realized
that he was lost. He wouldn't *say* he was lost because, well, he's a
guy, but he was lost just the same. Now, if being lost in the jungle
wasn't frightening enough to give Allen the yips, he was hiking
through an area known for, among other things, packs of wild
dogs. And it was getting dark.

As Dr. Christenson struggled to find his way to the valley below,
he happened upon a Maya village consisting of a few huts. In front
of one of the huts stood a bench, and sitting on the bench were
the village elders. Rather than ask for directions (Allen's pressing
issue), he wisely and carefully started the conversation with what
is known as the "Maya Introduction Ritual."

With the Maya you can't just walk up to a stranger and say,
"Hello, I'm Allen, and I'm lost." Protocol demands that you first
introduce yourself and all of your known ancestors—along with
what they did during their lives. (Try doing *that* while worrying
about roving packs of wild dogs.)

After more than an hour of ancestral talk, Allen was finally able to ask for directions, but before he could get on his way, one of the elders asked him what had brought him to their village. Dr. Christenson explained that he had been compiling a dictionary of their language. His answer took the elders by complete surprise. They had known that the Spanish language could be written, but it had never occurred to them that the same was true for Mayan.

Allen assured them that not only was it possible, but the ancients had done so frequently. In fact, the land around them was replete with temples that contained a great deal of early Mayan writing.

"What did our ancestors have to say?" one of the elders asked. Allen happened to be carrying a translation of an important historical document, so he pulled it out and read it to them. The villagers sat in silence, eagerly listening. Tears ran down their cheeks as they heard for the first time the recorded wisdom of their much-honored ancestors. "Are there other words? Where can we find even more words?"

As Allen explained that scholars were working on translating other writings, one of the elders asked, "Could I speak to you while you write down my words—for my children in my language?"

"Yes," the others chimed in, "could you write our words?"

Allen didn't make it down the mountain that evening, and it wasn't because of the dogs. The villagers asked him to play the role of scribe, late into the night, as eager fathers composed words of wisdom to their offspring. Finally, the chief invited Allen into his hut where he privately composed a document for his son. The chief had already lost eleven children, and now his only remaining son had been struck down with tuberculosis. He wanted to write a message to him in his own tongue before the disease inevitably took him. He poured his heart out as Allen sat and wrote.

As I listened to Allen tell his story, I was intrigued to see that upon first learning of their long-lost written language, the villagers wanted to hear the words of their ancestors—to learn from the wisdom of the ages. Then they became consumed with the idea of writing down their own thoughts to benefit their children.

How different we are from these Maya villagers. For the Maya, who saw and heard the written word for the first time, the value of it was incalculable. To those of us who live in a veritable sea of text, the marginal utility of the next written word approaches zero.

Our indifference is understandable. Since a codified system can be applied to any and all words (including the list of ingredients on a box of Cocoa Puffs), most of us have developed methods to insulate ourselves from an unrelenting deluge of minutiae, sales pitches, and drivel. As a natural consequence of nearly drowning in the printed word, we also don't write very much.

Unlike the Maya elders who, after knowing of their written language for only a few minutes, had already composed heart-felt notes of love and advice to their children, few of us have done the same with our own offspring despite the fact that we have known how to write for decades.

Writing is no longer our medium of choice. As leaders we certainly don't write serious thought pieces or calls to action as part of our routine. As parents, we are similarly stingy when it comes to writing words of adoration or instruction to our children. We also don't write our stories.

Today, when we do write, we compose e-mails, text messages, tweets, and such—often unpunctuated and almost always brief. The coin of today's verbal realm is idle chitchat, acronyms (LOL), and abbreviated business-speak. When we do write something of substance, it tends to be more technical than lyrical or heartfelt.

To put this change in communication style into perspective, consider the fact that Thomas Jefferson wrote more than twenty thousand letters during his career. Perhaps we don't match Jefferson's enthusiasm or pace because we've been punished for writing since childhood. I remember what it was like in school when my first attempts to capture my thoughts on paper fell under the chilling gaze of grammarians who accused me of dangling my modifiers and splitting my infinitives. That alone put me off writing for decades.

Irrespective of the reasons behind our reticence, the day will come when the primary artifacts we'll leave behind will be photographs, video clips, and written words. This means many of our offspring will know what we looked like at birthday parties (as seen in photos) as well as what we sounded like when giving advice to newlywed couples (as recorded on video). Sadly, since we've written little of any substance, they'll know almost nothing about our thoughts, beliefs, dreams, and feelings. They won't know our stories. They won't know us.

The Maya villagers that Allen chanced upon that evening understood the importance of the written word so clearly that they immediately wanted to apply their new knowledge. They shared their own thoughts with their children.

And now, through their eyes, I'm coming to the same understanding.

Perhaps I'll write a story or two.

SECTION

1

FAMILY LESSONS

THE GRAY FEDORA

"You don't have to assume the worst about everyone . . . The world isn't always out to get you."

SARAH DESSEN

In 1954, if you happened to be eight years old, and I was, Roy Rogers sat smack dab in the center of your universe. He was this marvelous cowboy/actor who was always chasing down the bad guys and saving the schoolmarm in the most remarkable and self-less ways. So, when the newspaper announced that there would be a Roy Rogers double feature showing on Saturday, I could hardly wait.

At that stage in my life, each weekday as I'd come home from school I'd stop off at my grandpa's place and talk with him about Trigger, Bullet, and the other members of Roy Rogers's entourage. Grandpa had never seen the singing cowboy in action, but he always showed great interest in whatever caught my attention. He would patiently listen to me as I retold each tale of derring-do. It was he who bought me my first Roy Rogers cap gun and holster.

In truth, while it was Roy who had captured my eight-year-old interest, it was Grandpa who had captured my heart. At five-foot-four with a fireplug shape and an amazing wit, Grandpa cut a large swath in my world. He owned and operated the neighborhood grocery store, and as far as my friends and I were concerned, that made him a celebrity. The fact that he was the guy who stood behind the *candy* counter—well, that made him a hero.

Like all septuagenarians of the time, whenever Grandpa went outside he wore a suit and hat. To him, you weren't fit for public appearance if you weren't in a wool suit. Furthermore, your suit would be incomplete if you didn't have a hat. In Grandpa's case, it was a gray fedora.

The day of the double feature finally arrived, and I stopped by Grandpa's store to let him know I'd be catching the bus that stopped in front of his place in order to go downtown and see Roy in action. He smiled broadly and explained that he too would be going into the city to stock up on supplies at the wholesale house. Maybe we'd run into each other. With the prospect of bumping into my grandfather firmly fixed in my mind, I headed off to the much-anticipated double feature.

Later that afternoon, after Roy had sung *Happy Trails* for the last time, I scurried to the bus stop a few blocks away and was forever changed. While sucking on a Tootsie Pop and still musing about Roy's latest conquest, I was accosted by an image that stopped me in my tracks. The Tootsie Pop fell from my mouth as I stood agape. There, at the end of the block, no more than twenty yards away, lay Grandpa on the sidewalk. He appeared to be dead. His body lay askew while his withered right hand clutched a brown paper bag. What had happened? Had Grandpa had a heart attack on the way to the wholesale house?

As I drew closer to Grandpa my fear turned to confusion and despair. Why was nobody helping him? It was a busy Saturday afternoon, and dozens of people were walking right past him without a glance. Nobody was lending Grandpa a hand. Had the world gone mad? Were there no heroes in Bellingham? Roy Rogers went toe-to-toe with bank robbers and cattle rustlers in order to right a wrong; couldn't somebody stop and help Grandpa?

When I finally fell to my knees next to Grandpa and brushed aside the fedora that was covering his face, I discovered that it wasn't Grandpa after all. It was a stranger—an old man who hadn't shaved in days, who smelled of wine, and who wasn't dead, but dead *drunk*. I recoiled from the stranger—as if bitten by a snake.

And then a warm wave of relief rolled over me. It wasn't Grandpa, and he wasn't dead! It wasn't Grandpa! I stood there and cried tears of sheer joy until a kindly lady stopped and asked if I needed help. I explained that I was okay and scampered off to catch the bus.

As I rode home, I realized that I had equated a fedora with Grandpa. So when I saw a man wearing Grandpa's hat of choice, I made a logical leap that caused me a great deal of grief. I wouldn't make that mistake again. Then my emotions darted in another direction as my wide-eyed innocence took over. Sure, this stranger wasn't *my* grandfather, but surely he was *someone's* grandfather. Where were his grandkids? And the people who passed by—why hadn't they done anything? I sobbed for the stranger all the way home.

When I finally burst through the front door of our brown clapboard house, I told my mom how I thought Grandpa had been dead and how it had turned out to be somebody else. She nodded knowingly and explained that the unfortunate fellow I had stumbled upon was a street person who was probably sleeping it off.

"But where were his grandkids?" I asked. Where was the little boy who would fall to his knees, hold him in his arms, and help him home? Mom didn't have an answer.

I was forever changed that day. First, I had opened the door into a part of life my parents had protected me from. Some people become indigents and live and die on the street. Worse still, we don't always know what to do about it. The second lesson I learned was life-changing. I discovered that if I put Grandpa's gray fedora on a stranger—instantly transforming him or her into a person I dearly loved—the stranger became someone worthy of my care and attention.

Putting a face on the faceless masses, learning the name of a crime or war victim, thinking of the people who cause you grief as decent human beings—well, this humanizing act has a dramatic impact on how you first think about and then treat others.

So, the next time you're feeling indignant or angry toward another person, put a fedora on him or her. Humanize that person by asking, "Why would a reasonable, rational, and decent person do that?" Not only will your feelings toward him or her change, but so will your actions. You'll become a far more caring, empathetic, and influential person. All through the aid of a fedora.

VIDEO: Watch Kerry Patterson tell the story of "The Gray Fedora"

To access a live-action portrayal of "The Gray Fedora" short story, told by Kerry himself, as well as other free resources, visit **www.vitalsmarts.com/bookresources**.

THIS IS ROCKET SCIENCE

//

"Intellectual growth should commence at
birth and cease only at death."

ALBERT EINSTEIN

W hen I woke up that morning, I never suspected that I'd burn
down my bedroom. But, then again, some days just don't go
as planned. It was a Sunday, and this meant that later that evening
the entire Patterson clan would plop down in front of their black-
and-white nineteen-inch DuMont TV and worship at the altar of
The Ed Sullivan Show.

We could hardly wait. Mr. Sullivan didn't merely entertain us; he
connected us backwoods Puget Sounders with the outside world.
Who knew what luminaries would beam into our home! Would it
be Elvis or maybe even the Beatles? Surely the ventriloquist Señor
Wences or the puppet Topo Gigio would grace the stage.

It was Sunday, it was sunny, and all was well.

And then came the bad news. Mom sat me down and explained
that she and Dad would be attending a meeting that evening and
that I'd have to chaperone in their stead. Chaperone? I was a fourteen-year-old kid. Whom was I supposed to chaperone?

Mom explained that one of the college girls who lived in the
boardinghouse our family owned and operated at the time wanted
to buy an insurance policy. Mom had volunteered both me and
our living room for the sales presentation. If listening to an insur-

ance salesman wasn't bad enough, the meeting was to take place during the sacred time slot of *The Ed Sullivan Show*.

When the appointed hour finally rolled around, I squirmed impatiently while the insurance fellow yammered on about "contingencies" and "risk aversion" until I could take it no longer. When the guy looked away to find a brochure, I quickly slipped into my bedroom adjacent to the living room. This put me out of range of the insurance talk, but with nothing to do.

Then it hit me. Under my desk was a large bowl of powdered rocket fuel I had recently concocted. Now would be the perfect time to turn it from loose powder into a solid mass by melting it down and letting it solidify. A solid mass, I had been told, would burn more evenly. Unfortunately, I didn't have the necessary equipment to perform this stabilizing task, so I quickly fashioned a Bunsen burner out of materials I found in the bathroom. A petroleum jelly lid, a wad of cotton, and a couple of jiggers of my dad's aftershave lotion—and *voilà*! I was ready to cook.

Next, I poured a generous portion of the powdered fuel into an empty chemical container that consisted of a cardboard tube with a flat metal bottom. The cardboard would provide me with a safe place to grip the container, while the metal bottom would take the heat from the flame.

Soon, I was holding the jury-rigged cauldron above the Aqua Velva flame and merrily melting the powder. Yes, I'd be missing Ed Sullivan's guest star, Richard Burton, as he performed a number from *Camelot*, but I was advancing science. What could be more important?

Then, with no warning whatsoever, the powder hit its ignition point and burst into a frightening torrent of flames, blasting the wallpaper above my desk and scorching a large patch of the ceiling. I couldn't drop the blazing tube, or it would have careened around the room and set the place on fire. So I gritted my teeth and held the cylinder firmly through its entire burn. For nearly a minute the fiery tube charred the wallpaper while dropping blazing debris on my arms and legs—burning holes in my shirt and pants and leaving behind pea-sized burns in my forearms and thighs.

The rest is a blur. When it was finally safe to set the container down, I bolted from my bedroom and threw open the front door to vent the house. Within minutes a fire truck rolled into our driveway. Seeing that the door was open, the firemen rushed in, assessed the danger, and started yelling at me for being so stupid as to . . . well, cook rocket fuel in my bedroom. Finally, one of them shook his index finger at me and shouted, "Kid, you're going to get it when your parents come home!"

Then my parents came home.

Watching a fire crew pull away from your home is never a good sign when you're the parent of a teenage boy. As Mom and Dad walked apprehensively into my bedroom and surveyed the damage, Mom stated, "You realize that you're going to have to set this right." (I did. I paid for the repairs out of my savings.)

And then Mom said something that was so quintessentially "Mom" that I've never forgotten it: "What did you learn from this adventure?"

When faced with the smoldering shell of a bedroom, most parents would have wanted a pound of flesh—or at least a good eight ounces. Mom marched to the beat of a different drummer. She wanted to know what I had learned from the incident. It wasn't a trick on her part; it was how Mom treated debacles. For her, every calamity was a learning opportunity, every mishap a chance to glean one more morsel of truth from the infinitely instructive universe.

So I talked to Mom and Dad about ignition points and research design as well as the need to take more precautions and seek stricter adult supervision. I even followed my own advice and never again blew up anything that wasn't mostly on purpose— save for one minor incident a few months later during a routine rocket test where I accidentally blew off my eyebrows. No big deal. Eyebrows grow back.

The good news is that I walked away from the flaming fuel incident with a deeper understanding of Mom's philosophy. She wanted me and my brother to be full-time learners—ambulant scholars, if you like. It was her mission in life to turn us into scientists who learned at every turn.

While your average citizen might bump into the world, take the occasional licking, and then endlessly complain, my mother wanted us to bounce back with the question: What does this teach us? While others carped about effects, Mom wanted us to find causes. In her view, our classroom needed to extend beyond the halls of academia and down any path our journey might take us— even into the occasional charred bedroom.

This isn't to suggest that either the home or the corporate learning environment should allow individuals to run about willy-nilly. I had been irresponsible, and I was held accountable. I had also been experimenting with rocket science, and Mom didn't want to stifle that part of me. She wanted me to experiment, and this called for calculated risks. She saw it as her job to teach me how to make the calculations and mitigate the risks, not to set aside my test tubes and chemicals. And definitely not to stop being a learner.

So let's take our lead from Mom and all of the other ambulant scholars out there. Should our best-laid plans run afoul, may we have the wisdom to pause, take a deep breath, and ask: What did we learn from this?

That is, right after we put out the flames.

THE MARSHMALLOW MASSACRE

//

"Last night, I dreamed I ate a ten-pound marshmallow.
When I woke up, the pillow was gone."

TOMMY COOPER

F irst dates can be tricky. If you don't act all prissy and polite, the whole thing can tank. I should know; mine was a real stinker. That's not to say that it didn't start out okay. A girl from my high school agreed to go to a party with me so I wasn't forced to ask a cousin. Always a plus. When we danced, she was only three inches taller than I. That was lucky. For the real bonus, my upper lip wasn't sporting its usual oozing cold sore. Call it kismet.

Alas, the magic didn't last. After dancing for only a few minutes, couples started to sneak into dark corners to make out—which seemed normal to me but really infuriated one of the chaperones. Like Batman dropping into Gotham City, Chaperone Guy leapt into the center of the rumpus room, flicked on the lights, and shouted, "It's game time!"

The kids who had been necking found this offer rather corny and unappealing, but to me it sounded terrific. My prospects for getting a kiss were nonexistent, and I was running dangerously low on small talk. Besides, I figured that if I won a party game my date would be impressed. Was that asking too much?

Apparently it was.

For the first game, the boys were asked to hold their hands behind their backs. Then they were supposed to eat six marshmallows attached four inches apart on a string that hung from the ceiling. This was terrific news. I was born to compete in just such an event. I loved sugar, and wolfing down food without the aid of my hands . . . well, let's put it this way: it wasn't entirely foreign to me.

When the gun sounded, I tore into my string of Jet-Puffed treats like a jackal into a springbok. My competitors were far less worried about winning than they were about appearing well mannered. They merely nibbled on their first marshmallow—occasionally dabbing their lips to maintain their proper appearance.

What a rout. I gobbled my way straight up my assigned string and swallowed all six spongy confections in about thirty seconds. When I raised my arms in victory, all eyes turned to me in disbelief. Nobody could fathom that I had already finished all six marshmallows. Then their looks turned from surprise to confusion to disgust.

I couldn't figure what had gone wrong. Why were they gawking at me as if I'd just dropped my retainer in the punch bowl? Then I caught a glimpse of myself in the mirror. Oops. Not only had I swallowed the marshmallows, I had swallowed the string as well. Hanging out of the corner of my mouth was six inches of unswallowed evidence.

"Now what?" I thought to myself. Then, I recalled my ninth-grade health class, where I had learned that swallowing a string was likely to wreak havoc with your bowels. I needed to retrieve it—and pronto. Regrettably, it never occurred to me to do so in the privacy of a bathroom. Instead, I yanked the string out of my gullet in full public view.

The act of fishing a string from my stomach probably wouldn't have been entirely repulsive were it not for the marshmallows. They came back with the string—dripping with the Orange Nehi soda I had guzzled as a precompetition pick-me-up—six candied corpses on the rebound.

I also hadn't counted on a group of muscles at the end of my esophagus that—in trapdoor fashion—work to keep food inside one's stomach, where it belongs. As I awkwardly pulled on the string, the trapdoor grabbed on to each marshmallow. In the end, not only did I yank back a ghastly mass of slime and goo, I retched as each marshmallow fought the esophageal sentinels.

The overall effect wasn't good. I pulled on the string—choking, spitting, retching, and gagging. The crowd looked on in disgust. Except for the boys. Once the boys decided that yanking a string from one's stomach had "athletic event" written all over it, they cheered the appearance of each returning marshmallow as if they were witnessing a fullback breaking through the line of scrimmage.

Yank, gag, cheer. Yank, gag, cheer. The boys couldn't get enough of it. The girls not so much. They viewed the whole affair with something less than admiration. They saw neither the athleticism nor the wonder in my retrieval trick. Reeling from the sight of slime and goo, they covered their eyes, backed off in horror, and raced for the bathroom. Eventually, my date left with a friend.

Oh yes, my first date was a genuine debacle. As I lay awake that night trying to figure out where I had gone wrong, it came to me in a flash. The fact that I had choked on the string was not the problem. Okay, it was *a* problem, but not *the* problem. What had really gone haywire was my thought process. I had concluded in my seventeen-year-old brain that my date would admire what I admired. I believed that she would be impressed with my talent for wolfing down marshmallows and then, as a bonus, retrieving them from my gut—despite the resistance of an uncooperative esophagus. The guys were impressed. *I* was impressed. Surely my date would be impressed.

As luck would have it, the girl I had asked to the party marched to the beat of a different drummer. She wasn't interested in hanging out with Psycho Marshmallow Boy. She was actually sickened by my performance.

The point is, I sought to give my date something she didn't want. I looked into her heart and found my own desires—much like the time, a few years later, when I gave my wife a first-rate stereo system that I had been coveting for months.

"Look at that beauty!" I shouted as my wife unwrapped the gift. "An eight-track cartridge stereo with locking fast forward. Complete with analog VU level meters!"

"Well, here's *your* birthday present," my wife scowled, "Where's *mine?*"

Busted.

So, what should we learn from this fiasco besides "Don't retrieve a string from your stomach in full public view"? It's this. Before you do something for—or give something to—another person, learn what *they* value. Don't assume that what's good for you, the goose, is good for him or her, the gander. Learn the true meaning of the Golden Rule: Do unto others as they would have you do unto them, not as you would do unto yourself.

And trust me on this one. If you don't get it right, you'll be taking back that eight-track stereo for sure. Complete with analog VU level meters.

WHOSE LINE IS IT ANYWAY?

//

"You can observe a lot by just watching."

YOGI BERRA

It was a Saturday morning in the summer of 1980. The front doorbell chimed, and my seven-year-old daughter, Rebecca, ran to see who was there. It turned out to be her best friend, Candy, who smiled and asked, "Can you come out and play?" Rebecca took a quick look at her pal, curled her lip, said "No," and then slammed the door.

I was watching and thought to myself, *who slams the door in a friend's face? Apparently my daughter does.* So I asked her what had just taken place. She explained that her mom had told her to clean her room before she went anywhere.

"So you wanted to play, but you had to clean your room first," I carefully paraphrased. "Yes," she responded. "The sooner I do my chores, the sooner I can play."

"How do you think Candy felt about your slamming the door in her face?" I asked.

"She looks sad," Rebecca explained as we peered out the window and watched Candy trudge back to her house. "I guess I hurt her feelings."

"Can you think of something you could have said that would have been kinder?" I inquired.

Rebecca had no answer. That's because she's human, and we humans aren't born with much knowledge. We certainly aren't born with the complicated, and often subtle, skills that make up social awareness and charm.

Unlike some guppies Rebecca and I had watched being born a few days earlier, humans don't arrive with knowledge about anything. Guppies shoot out of their moms like a mini-torpedo, take a quick look around, swim to the nearest plant, hide in the foliage, and then swim in sync with the moving vegetation. They're born with first-class hiding skills. That's because the fish around them (including Daddy and Uncle Guppy) eat baby guppies. To maintain the species, guppies are taught most of what they'll need to survive—not in schools (pun intended), but in-utero. They're born teenagers. Most of what they'll ever know they know at birth.

Humans, in contrast, are born with a blank slate. Infants know nothing, nor are they preprogrammed to do anything. The good news: humans don't get jerked around by instincts. (Hey, let's swim up an Alaskan stream until we beat ourselves to death on the rocks!) The bad news: humans have to learn how to survive—skill by skill, situation by situation. Social scripts are no exception. By age seven, Rebecca hadn't learned the door script yet and was having a hard time inventing one of her own.

So I continued the instruction. "What if you said, 'I'd love to come out and play, but I have to clean my room first. When I finish I'll come over and get you'?"

Next, I stepped outside and knocked on the door. Rebecca answered, and I asked her to come out and play. At this point in the story I typically ask audiences what they think Rebecca did. They respond, "She slammed the door in your face!" They're wrong. Rebecca politely said, "I'd love to come out and play, but I have to clean my room first. When I'm done I'll come get you." In less than three minutes, I had taught Rebecca a social script.

While working as a professor a few months later, I decided to test whether I could apply what I had done with a seven-year-old to grown adults by teaching them a social script. And unlike Rebecca, whom I taught openly and to her knowledge, I wanted to see if I could teach adults a social script without them even noticing.

To find out, I asked a group of graduate students to cut into movie theater lines. Our goal was to count how many people would typically say something to the line-cutter. In the laid-back Mountain West, where we conducted the experiment, no matter the gender, size, or demeanor of the line-cutter, nobody spoke up. Better to stay mum, the subjects concluded, and avoid any potential conflict.

Next, I asked the students to cut in front of not a stranger, but a fellow student whom we'd secretly placed in line. The student was instructed to become upset. "Hey, quit cutting in line!" the student would brusquely say to the cutter, who would then go to the end of the queue.

Next, we waited a minute and cut in front of the person standing *behind* the student who had just chewed out the line-cutter. Would experimental subjects be informed and emboldened from the demonstration they had just witnessed and now speak their minds? Since we hadn't exhibited a very healthy script, we hypothesized that most people would remain silent. And they did. Not one person spoke harshly after watching someone else do the same.

For our third trial, we cut in front of a student who was instructed to be diplomatic. The student was to smile and say, "I'm sorry. Perhaps you're unaware. We've been waiting in line for more than fifteen minutes." The cutter would then apologize and go to the end of the line.

Now for the big question. Similar to Rebecca learning the door script, would onlookers learn and use their new and smart-sounding line-cutting script? We waited a minute, cut in front of the subject standing behind the positive role model, and watched what took place—in fifty different lines. The results were startling. More than 80 percent of the people who had observed the effective interaction spoke up. In fact, they said the exact same words they had heard modeled. We had done it! By using a positive role model, we had taught strangers a social script that they immediately put into action. And we had done it without them even knowing.

The implications of this research are obvious. Humans, despite the fact that they're born without a scrap of useful knowledge, can observe, learn, and put into play a whole host of skills—including social scripts. For example, you watch an employee argue for his idea in a meeting with far too much force, causing others to resist. You note that the tactic didn't work. Then you watch someone tentatively present the same idea and ask others what they think—this approach is met with acceptance. *That nonaggressive approach worked!* you think to yourself, and, just like Rebecca, you've now learned a new social tactic.

And yet, most of us spend little time observing, learning, and teaching social scripts. We exert more effort learning French (or even Klingon) than studying human interaction. But this can change simply by watching people in tough social interactions, spotting what works and what doesn't, and then practicing the skills yourself. Eventually, you can teach the skills to others.

Don't rely on chance—certainly not with your children, friends, and coworkers. Expecting people to invent tactics for working through complex social issues is akin to handing a child a pencil and paper and expecting him to invent calculus. Instead, take what you've learned through observing others, break it into component skills, and teach these social snippets to those around you. Teaching others social skills is one of the best gifts you can give them. Plus, if you get *really* good at handling high-stakes conversations, you no longer have to put up with line-cutters.

ONE-TOOTH REE

//

"I'm on the Internet. I stay informed. They let
old people on the Internet, you know."

STEPHEN EMOND

As I walked into church one Sunday, my neighbors Betsy and
Howard Nielson greeted me warmly at the door. Howard had
been a chemistry professor and Betsy an attorney. Both had been
retired for about five years. When I first met them at a neighborhood gathering, I discovered they had lived in the Bay Area in the
early 70s—the same time I had been stationed there in the Coast
Guard.

As we shared memories of the area, the conversation turned to
the marvelous regional theater. I enthusiastically explained that
one of the highlights of my stay in California had been a local
theater competition I had attended. The theme had been "One,
Two, Three." One of the ten-minute skits that competed was aptly
retitled *One-Tooth Ree*. It was about a poor fellow named Ree who
had but one tooth and the challenges he faced trying to find a girl-
friend. The music, lyrics, script, and staging were delightful, and I
gushed over its creativity.

"One-Tooth Ree!" Howard exclaimed. "Why, Betsy wrote the
play, the music, and the lyrics. I did the sets and staging." Somehow, after thirty years of moving about the country, I had stumbled across the people who had written and produced an obscure
mini-musical I had adored. The three of us laughed about the coin-

cidence, and I marveled that a chemist and lawyer had crafted such an incredible production. Both were modest in their responses and eventually went on to talk about their other surprise talents—the sculpting awards he had won and the books she had written.

"Actually, I've written quite a lot," Betsy enthused, "but nowadays nobody asks me about my work."

From there, the conversation turned to the fact that the Nielsons felt they were being put out to pasture—despite the fact that they wanted to remain yoked. As they turned sixty, they had been given the bum's rush at work and now, within their own church group, they had been assigned more modest responsibilities. Two vibrant parishioners, who had once run the charity drives and led the youth camping programs, had been politely released from their jobs and appointed "greeters."

"It's a token job," Betsy explained with a wry smile. "You can't exactly fire people at church, so you make up some position and move them to that."

"Not that people don't need to be greeted," Howard added. "It's just that we have so much more to offer."

How must it feel to be bubbling over with ideas and rarely asked for your point of view? What's it like to stand on the sidelines and crave to be sent back into the game? *Put me in coach*, you think to yourself. *I can do it!* But the coach never looks your way.

Taking my cue from the Nielsons, I started making it a point to talk to older people I ran into at church and around the neighborhood—no longer making small talk—but *big* talk. After exchanging greetings, I would ask, "What's the most interesting thing you learned in your career?" or "What advice do you have for me as a new grandparent?" or "What's the most important book you ever read?"

From there, the discussion always turns lively and interesting. It's as if you unlock the door to a living library. For instance, last week when my neighbor Henry (a retired geologist) stopped by to take a look at our remodeling project, I took him over to our new granite countertops and asked him to educate me about the stone.

"If I were still teaching geology," Henry enthused, "I'd bring my students by your place just to look at this! Examining this stone," Henry continued, "is like reading an ancient manuscript. The granite you see in the field is covered with dirt, and even when it's exposed, it's still hard to examine. When you slice and polish a massive piece like this, you can peer back into the very formation of the earth.

"For example, you see this dark brown scar that runs across this slab? The stone had a crack in it and millennia ago, magma poured into the void. And you see these tiny marks that look like ancient writing? They're called 'glyphs.' It all starts when . . ."

It was fascinating.

Inspired by my conversation with Henry, I decided to ask Betsy Nielson to share some of her writing with me. She had suggested that nobody asked her about her work anymore, so I asked her.

Within hours, Betsy appeared at our door with a large book in hand. She reverently opened it to a picture of a young man standing at attention in full flight gear. It was her brother Roy, and he had just graduated from flight school.

"In this book," Betsy explained, "I contributed a story about my brother Roy's flight experience in World War II."

Then I noticed Betsy cradling a letter in her hands—holding it more like a religious artifact than a sheet of paper.

"It's a letter Roy sent me," Betsy said as she fought back a tear. "It starts out, 'Dear Sis.'" She then paused to regain her composure. "Roy was eight years my senior and thoughtful enough to write his kid sister about once a month. Receiving a letter from him was a special event. In this particular letter, Roy talks about what's going on that week and ends by hoping that his flight scheduled for later that day will be successful. He and his crew were hunting down enemy submarines, and that was always dangerous."

"So what happened?" I asked.

"You'll note the date on the letter." Betsy answered. "It was the last day of the war."

"And?"

"And Roy's plane was shot down. He and his entire crew were lost. My brother and his buddies were among the last soldiers to die. They may have been *the* last soldiers to lose their lives in the war."

No wonder Betsy was cradling the letter. It was a poignant and tender piece of history. Tears ran down our cheeks as we discussed Roy's sacrifice and Betsy's feelings. It was a cherished moment for me, and it had been the result of asking a simple question: "Would you share some of your writings?" I had called Betsy back into the game, and both of us were blessed for my having done so.

It had been easy to unlock this living library. All I did was take the time to chat with an older friend. And when I did, I switched from small talk to big talk. Then I was privileged to listen to her marvelous story.

In Betsy's own words, unlocking untold treasures had been as simple as *one-tooth ree.*

THE HOLE IN OUR BACKYARD

///////////////////////////////////////

"It is interesting that we call something good a 'dream,'
but being called a 'dreamer' is somewhat of a putdown."

VERA NAZARIAN

Sometimes when I wake up in the morning it's 1957, and I'm eleven years old. This illusion is rooted in a time from my preteen years, when my dad held a job at the local plywood plant by day and collected payments on magazine subscriptions by night. Between the two jobs, Dad earned enough money to put our family about three slices of baloney above the poverty line. Meaning that we lived down a long, pot-holed road in an unadorned, one-bedroom house so small that your average NBA center could stretch out his arms and span the entire living room.

But Dad had more than two jobs; he also had Mom, who had big plans for escaping our tiny home and settling into something "more suitable."

Our climb up the social ladder didn't come easily. After attempting several failed home businesses, Mom read an ad in the local paper placed by an elderly couple who wanted to sell their college boardinghouse. The 1880s estate they were putting up for sale sat on the border of the local college and housed thirteen coeds. The two owners had worked the facility for more than three decades and were now ready to retire.

Mom, seeing a lifeline, borrowed our neighbor's car, drove to the boardinghouse, met with the aging couple, and talked them into lending her and Dad money so that they could then make a down payment on the house.

"It's easy," I remember Mom enthusing. "All I have to do is cook breakfast and dinner for seventeen people (the boarders, plus our family) seven days a week. How hard could that be?" A few weeks after inking the deal, Mom arose at 6:00 a.m. and made breakfast for seventeen—which included throwing bacon on the grill at 6:20 a.m.

After a week of this routine, the smell of frying bacon awakened me just in time to complete my assigned task of setting the table. To this day, when someone rises early and cooks bacon, I wake up thinking it's 1957.

Thanks to Mom's dream, our little family climbed out of our tiny hovel in the woods and into a boardinghouse downtown. Despite our move up the ladder, there still was never any money left for luxuries such as vacations and college funds, and I was now a preteen with an eye set on a higher education. So Mom put me to work painting the exterior of the entire boardinghouse—four hours per day, every weekday, for three summers.

"I'll pay you when you graduate from high school and we send you off to college," Mom explained one day when I had the temerity to ask to be paid for the work I was doing.

But how would my folks earn the college funds they had promised me, given that they hadn't been able to put any money aside so far? At first, Mom made wedding cakes. That was a lot of work for little money. She needed to dream bigger. And then it hit her. She now lived next to a college—why not take classes? So, in 1964, when I graduated from high school, Mom graduated from college and took a full-time job as an elementary school teacher, where she generated, as promised, any college funds I lacked.

Of course, not all of Mom's dreams panned out. After visiting my parents' new home in Glendale, Arizona, between semesters from college, I discovered another of her plans. "What's the hole in the backyard?" I asked.

"I'm digging a swimming pool," Mom explained with a straight face. She and Dad didn't have the money to build a pool, but if Mom dug a hole, then maybe they'd find a way to complete the job. Always the dreamer.

A few days later, I overheard a woman at church asking who my mother was. Another congregant explained, "She's that crazy lady with the hole in her backyard." Apparently, word of Mom's harebrained scheme had spread. What middle-aged woman digs a swimming pool with a hand shovel? It turns out, her detractors were right. Mom never did finish the pool. In fact, she never even finished the hole.

Throughout her life, Mom, despite her best intentions, dug a lot of holes. And as you'd suspect, she also had a lot of critics. "You'll never be able to buy a boardinghouse. You have no money." "You'll never be able to retire to Mexico. How will you get there?" "You'll never, you'll never, you'll never . . ."

Sometimes they were right. Years of cooking for seventeen people generated no savings. Baking dozens of wedding cakes resulted in little money. And then there was always that hole in the backyard. People who only saw that pit and knew nothing of Mom's more successful endeavors thought she was zany—even irresponsible.

In her defense, Mom wasn't your high-profile dreamer. She wasn't a Cinderella who (as was the case with most storybook heroines) dreamed of the day she would be rescued from her plight and taken away to live in a glorious mansion where she would live happily ever after.

Mom never asked or expected to be rescued. All she asked for was a chance to work her way to a better station in life. Her dreams always included her and Dad (and often me and my brother) entering new circumstances and then working our way to the next rung up the ladder.

And so I share this story to honor my mother and others like her. For those who dare not only to dream, but also to fight to make those dreams come true—despite the naysayers and set-backs. I give my respect to those who doggedly create one more dream, because, unlike many of us, they look back on their lives and see the fruits of their efforts—not merely the holes in the backyard.

STAY AWAY FROM THE CHURNING WATERS

///

"If called by a panther, don't anther."

OGDEN NASH

When my best friends and I were kids growing up along the shores of Puget Sound, the water was our favorite playground. Hardly a summer day passed that we didn't find a way to float in it. By age fourteen, my friends and I had widened our tastes from floating safely in placid lagoons to using the water as a thrill park—particularly the water found underneath the docks. This was back in the early 60s, when fish canneries sat perched on docks high above the bay and spewed a ghastly stream of cast-off salmon heads and slimy innards straight into the water below. Sharks gathered at the entry point of the disgusting flow in a feeding frenzy of pink froth, teeth, and terror.

Few people have ever seen a sight such as the one beneath those canneries. Few people would *want* to see such a sight. Unless, of course, you're a fourteen-year-old boy and pretty much live for the chance to throw yourself smack-dab in the middle of a biological freak show. Which is exactly who we were and what we did. My buddies and I took one look at the tangle of teeth and fins and knew we had to find a way to experience it up close.

After scrounging driftwood and small pieces of rope for a couple of days, our intrepid gang cobbled together a raft for just such idiotic purposes. We christened our craft "Death" and then promptly paddled straight to the heart of the toothy treasure.

It's hard to describe the sheer visceral pleasure of gliding into a foaming pool of frenzied sharks. There we were, surrounded by a pulsating mass of fins, teeth, and eyeballs—completely swallowed up by the roar of gushing entrails raining down from the canneries above. It was fourteen-year-old heaven.

At first, we just stood there, triumphantly ensconced in the epicenter of this ecological nightmare. And then, one part adrenaline, two parts testosterone, and ten parts boy took over. First, we smacked the throbbing mass with our paddles. Take that, you nasty sharks! Smack! Smack! Smack! Then we poked the finned beasts with assorted sticks. Poke. Poke. Poke. We capped off this attack with a series of whoops and grins—shouting and gyrating on the very edge of sanity. It was a perfect teenage boy moment.

And then, with one misplaced foot, everything changed. Rudy stepped over the edge and tumbled into the churning waters. Movies generally show such heart-stopping moments in slow motion. That's because in real life they *happen* in slow motion. When Rudy fell, time stopped. First, Rudy's left leg slipped off the edge. Then his body hung in the space between the raft and the danger below for what seemed forever. He hovered in the air in a grotesque, cartoon-like position until he finally lurched toward the outstretched hands of his friends. As he cleared the raft, the back of his head found the outside log with a sickening thud. Rudy was out like a light, floating in a boil of ichthyoidal rage.

And then, a hero was born. Pete, dressed only in ragged cutoff jeans and a T-shirt, jumped into the frenetic foam without so much as a thought for his own safety. It was heart-stopping to watch him leap straight into the jaws of death. True, the Puget Sound sharks weren't thirty-foot great whites. Maybe they were only four to six feet long, but their teeth were dangerous enough. Somehow, Pete managed to pull himself and Rudy back onto the raft, but not before both had received several scrapes. For five minutes, we huddled together in a mist of foam, blood, fear, and gratitude. Then we slowly made our way back to shore.

For those of you who have never been a fourteen-year-old boy who has just escaped death by a whisker, you might think that we then triumphantly returned home. We didn't. Instead, we did what foolish boys like us have done for centuries. We came up with a cover story. We couldn't tell our moms that Rudy and Pete had fallen into a whirlpool of sharks. They would have asked awkward questions about where the sharks came from and how we got so close to them in the first place. So we made up a whopper, sneaked into Rudy's house, and ministered to the wounded.

Years passed, until one evening I told this story while standing around a campfire at a father-and-son outing. By the time I was through, the crowd was ready to erect a statue in honor of Pete's valor. In fact, I made all of us kids out to be a fanciful combination of swarthy adventurers and swashbuckling daredevils. Then, as I noticed my own boys hanging on my every word, I reversed course. I could see that they were just aching to swim with the sharks. They wanted their shot at becoming a hero.

Of course, this was the *last* thing I wanted them to do. So I added the following editorial comments: Many acts of heroism are immediately preceded by acts of utter insanity—requiring the very acts of heroism we're extoling in the first place. If we boys hadn't been so completely insane as to paddle straight into the middle of a roiling mass of feeding sharks and then jump and hoot and skip around until one of us fell in, we wouldn't have needed a hero.

Hero moments arise because it's not nearly as fun to avoid danger by a distance as it is to climb into the mouth of the grim reaper himself and then, at the very last second, scamper to safety in a flamboyant feat of athleticism. Now you've got yourself a story to tell.

Fortunately, when you're talking to your own children, reason prevails. You encourage your own offspring to avoid danger by a safe margin. With them, you give crystal-clear directions: You can go into the water. No problem there. Just don't swim into the churning waters. In fact, *don't go near* the churning waters.

I was reminded of this notion at work one day when, at the end of a sexual harassment seminar, one of the participants asked, "Can we still tell blonde jokes?" Another fellow chimed in with, "Yeah, and can I still tell a woman how good she looks in a sweater?"

Really? I thought. *Do you have to walk right up to the far edge of what is safe, tasteful, and reasonable and then lean out and peer into the abyss of lawsuits, humiliation, and shame? What are you, a perennial teenager?*

Stay away from tasteless actions, perilous tactics, and all behaviors that offer little and risk much. Stay away from fast-moving, toothy monsters. And most certainly don't poke them with sticks. Better yet, avoid danger by a healthy margin. Stay away from the churning waters.

HE GLOWS IN THE DARK

//

"As soon as there is life, there is danger."

RALPH WALDO EMERSON

One day, as my father sped along the expressway, I noticed from my position in the backseat that the door next to me was slightly ajar. I took one look at it and did what any ten-year-old kid would do—I grabbed the handle and tried to give the door a quick open and close. The instant the latch released, the door violently flew open and stretched me out like Stretch Armstrong, dangling me inches above the pavement. This happened (believe it or not) because the doors were designed to open backward. The instant you opened the door, the rushing air blew the door wide open and routinely yanked passengers onto the pavement.

Think about it. College-educated engineers—grown adults with children of their own—purposely designed doors that flew open in the wind. In fact, nearly every part found in a car built in that era was dangerous. Door pulls were veritable spears. The dashboard contained all kinds of pokey things that would leave ghastly impressions in your forehead at a time when seat belts weren't even an option.

Cars weren't the only source of danger kids faced in the 50s. About once a month my friends and I stopped by the Buster Brown shoe store to play with the x-ray machine placed prominently in the entrance. We, of course, weren't interested in seeing if our shoes fit. We took turns holding our hands, arms, legs, and yes, even our heads, in the foot space while a friend gawked at the glowing skeletal image. I'm fairly certain my buddies and I logged more than an hour's worth of electromagnetic radiation on the old shoe-fitting machine. Lucky us.

Your typical home wasn't much safer. On more than one occasion, I broke open thermometers and played with liquid mercury until the heavy metal was absorbed into my body, costing me—I'm fairly certain—a good two hundred points on the SAT. And let's not forget the marvelous chemistry set that my grandpa gave me for my birthday. It provided all the ingredients you needed for creating gunpowder, rocket fuel, flash bombs, and other such childhood delights.

I did get lucky in one regard. My parents decided that the "Atomic Energy Lab" that was also for sale at the time was too expensive to give me as a birthday gift. This children's toy came complete with a Geiger counter and (you're not going to believe this) samples of uranium and radium. As chance would have it, my parents were just a few dollars short of having a son who glowed in the dark.

Sometimes the ease with which we gained access to dangerous materials put our entire community at risk. For instance, I routinely toured naval vessels as a boy—whenever the fleet came to town. One year, while touring a gun ship, I snuck away from the tour group to find a place where I could examine cool navy stuff without being monitored. After a brief search, I holed up in one of the gun turrets, where I found a chair connected to an ocular device that gave me a close-up view of the hills overlooking the bay.

Wanting to see my own home, I carefully moved a couple of levers that changed the view—accompanied by an unidentified loud noise. After maneuvering the image for a minute or two, I finally had a close-up view of my own home on Garden Street.

Then, just as I was about to move the sighting device to spy on a neighbor, I was viciously yanked out of the seat by the scruff of my neck. It turns out I wasn't merely moving the gun sight when I jimmied those levers; I was moving an actual cannon. That's what was making the mysterious noise. A gunner's mate spotted the howitzer in motion, ran up to the turret, saw me (an eleven-year-old) aiming the gun at the hillside, and yanked me out of harm's way—nearly separating my head from the rest of my body.

The good news is that these are all examples taken from the 1950s when, apparently, children could easily be replaced and safety wasn't all that necessary. Today, we've made vast improvements in keeping heavy metals, dangerous chemicals, radioactive materials, electromagnetic beams, and howitzers out of the reach of children. We can all be thankful for that.

However, even in today's safety-conscious world where we've outlawed most of what I played with as a boy, there is a deadly and invisible force that can still be found in any gathering of two or more people. I'd like to point it out, so we can guard against its lethal effects.

I noticed this perilous force while watching a political debate. As I listened to individuals discuss what was happening in our country and why it was either positively brilliant or insanely stupid, I realized that as we unknowingly exposed ourselves to unseen dangers as kids, we are now being exposed to the killing effects of a whole new threat. We're exposed to the dangers of (drumroll, please) assuming our own omniscience.

Here's how this omniscience thing works. People talk about something as complicated as revamping the country's healthcare system as if their view is remarkably simple, totally correct, completely obvious, and recognized by all sentient beings. Their opponents' view, in contrast, is just plain stupid—so stupid, in fact, that you can't listen to his or her ludicrous assertions without rolling your eyes in utter disbelief.

Now, don't get me wrong; Unlike invisible radiation, you can hear and see the arguments people make. They generally say their arguments aloud and with great force. Sadly, the assumptions *behind* the arguments ("I'm smart and right, and you're stupid and wrong") often remain unseen and undiscussed. Such highly pernicious views provide such a killing blow to civil discourse that they need to be spotted, labeled, and put under lock and key.

Heaven only knows the effect assumed omniscience is having on today's youth. Children should be raised in an environment of passionate, transparent, *and civil* discourse, where all parties openly analyze arguments from all angles. Smugness needs to be replaced with humility, preening with listening, and certainty with curiosity.

That means we have to become less comfortable with black-and-white and more comfortable with gray. We need to admit that whenever there's a hard-to-resolve problem with thousands of people *on both sides* of the issue (all equally adamant about their view), there's a good chance that both sides of the argument have pluses and minuses. It's our job to find the best solutions by discovering a new or third way. We must find the truth wherever it lies.

Your kids may never be exposed to the home version of an atomic energy lab or allowed to play with the howitzers I seemed to find at every turn, but hardly a day passes that they (and you) aren't exposed to the deadly dangers of cocksure belief in overstated arguments. It falls on all of us to first highlight and then remove the danger. Help save yourself and the next generation from the dangerous effects of assumed omniscience. It's every bit as deadly as radium.

THE PATH TO HAPPINESS

"Sometimes I lie awake at night, and I ask, 'Where have I gone wrong?' Then a voice says to me, 'This is going to take more than one night.'"

CHARLES M. SCHULZ

When I was seven years old, I learned how to ride a bike on my brother's J. C. Higgins. It was a rusted-out, dilapidated wreck, but it ran okay and I wanted to ride it every chance I could get. I lay awake nights thinking about it. I was obsessed with it. Sadly, it was my older brother's pride and joy, so you can guess how that worked out for me. To be honest, given a choice, I would have preferred a twenty-six-inch, carbine-action Schwinn Tornado, but I would have settled for my brother's castoff wreck in a heartbeat.

Mom saw me eyeballing the Higgins for about the thousandth time and came up with a plan. As background: My grandmother had divorced my grandfather and married a wealthy lawyer who was so earnest in his desire to show his love for her that he gave her a two-hundred-pound industrial ironing machine. (And they say romance is dead.)

Grandma had other ideas. She figured she could use her new-found wealth to send her laundry not through a giant ironing machine, but to a place where *other* people would do the actual work.

"With your bad back and all," Grandma explained to my mother as two longshoremen wheeled the mammoth ironing machine into our home, "this beauty is just what the doctor ordered."

She was right. The machine was terrific—if you happened to work for Barnum and Bailey and needed to touch up a circus tent. Unfortunately, the thing was hard to operate, "ate" shirts and blouses, and only made Mom's back feel worse. Eventually, the monster was moved to our basement, where it sat next to my brother's bike—the one I so sorely coveted.

"I bet," Mom explained one night over dinner, "we could take that silly ironing machine that is just gathering dust in the basement and auction it off."

"We could certainly use the money," Dad replied.

"Yes, and I know just what to do with it. Billy has grown too big for his bike, so I figure we can sell the ironing machine at auction and then turn around and buy Billy a bigger, better bike."

This wasn't going well for me.

"And then Kerry can have Billy's old bike."

All right. I could live with that.

Two weeks later, when the local auctioneer placed the ironing machine up for bid, Dad explained that we needed to get about fifteen dollars if we expected to turn around and buy one of the bikes that was going up for auction. At first, the curious apparatus didn't get a single bid. The folks at the auction didn't know what to make of it. But then the auctioneer read the instructions from the metal plaque soldered to the body.

"Why, it's a fancy automatic ironing machine," he announced. Soon the bidding was off and running until a woman with a large feathered hat bid fifteen dollars.

"Sold!"

When we returned home later that day, my brother Billy jumped for joy at the sight of the secondhand Schwinn bike Dad had purchased for him with the auction money. Meanwhile, I rushed to the basement to claim my J. C. Higgins. I was ecstatic. At last, a bike of my own! Within seconds I hopped on the rusted hand-me-down and rode around the neighborhood shouting and yip-ping for joy. It was a dream come true. For about five minutes.

Then I realized that I didn't really have any place to go. (I was seven. Where would I go?) Nor did I have any smooth surfaces to take me there—just a bunch of rutted hills that led to more rutted hills. Plus, with only one gear, the Higgins was *really* hard to pedal. Oh, yes, and then there was the endless rain. You can't overestimate the buzz-killing power of a constant drizzle on a bike with no fenders. Within a month my long-coveted bike sat in the space left by the ironing machine until Mom eventually gave it to Goodwill.

This wasn't the last time I yearned for something I was convinced would bring me happiness, only to discover I was dead wrong. You'd think that after a string of disappointing purchases we'd all have learned that owning *things* doesn't exactly guarantee happiness.

Regrettably, each year, thousands of ads tell us that buying *things* will indeed bring us happiness—and possibly more. When I was a teenager, the makers of Brylcreem promised to make my hair so attractive that women would run their fingers through it. I'm still waiting. And then there was my first Slinky. How long can you play with a helical spring and still have fun? For me, ten minutes.

It's not as if having more stuff *never* helps. According to one study, happiness does go up with income—to a point. And then it levels off. Not having enough to pay for the necessities wears on you, so happiness rises with an infusion of cash. But when you reach a certain level of owning stuff, your happiness quotient stays the same. That is, unless you use that stuff to (1) create meaningful family experiences or (2) help others. Engage in either or both of these activities, and more money can indeed yield more happiness.

Last week I witnessed this for myself. My twelve-year-old granddaughter, Rachel, was dusting shelves for her mother while a friend stood by in tennis gear waiting to play doubles. Rachel's three-year-old sister, Lizzy, was toddling behind her, and after Rachel dusted each shelf, Lizzy would plead, "Help me!" Rachel would then lift Lizzy who, in turn, would drag her miniature duster over the same surface.

Given how little help Lizzy was providing, I thought Rachel would ditch her baby sister in favor of playing tennis. But she didn't. You could tell from the smile on her face that she took genuine pleasure from indulging her little sister.

"Rachel enjoys helping others more than doing just about anything," her mother explained. What a blessing to have learned at such a young age that serving others brings joy. Sadly, unless the world experiences some sort of cataclysmic upheaval in which singing the praises of "things" mysteriously comes to a screeching halt, one of the most important principles ever known to humankind will continue to remain largely unadvertised.

Of course, there's no knowing for sure. A giant ironing machine might be just what you need. Using the right hair cream might actually draw fingers to your hair. But then again, maybe these results won't feel all that wonderful. Most assuredly, none of them can be counted on to bring you anything as important as happiness.

You want happiness, and you want it fast? Well, it won't be that J. C. Higgins that will get you there—or a fancy sports car for that matter. Happiness is not about things, and it can't be achieved alone. Take your cue from Rachel. Use your time and resources to genuinely and freely serve others. Find a way to first bring others joy.

That's the path to happiness.

JUST A BOY

//

"It's not time to worry yet."

HARPER LEE, *TO KILL A MOCKINGBIRD*

Yesterday, when I stopped by our local pharmacy, I noticed a new addition to the staff. Working alongside an elderly gentleman and his adult son (both pharmacists) was a boy dressed in an apron—complete with a nametag announcing, "Hello, I'm Nate."

As I waited for my prescription, I struck up a conversation with the youngster and learned that he was, as I suspected, the owner's grandson. It was his first day on the job. Naturally, he wasn't allowed to go near the drugs. Nevertheless, he was doing his best to make a contribution.

"I loaded the cooler with drinks," Nate explained. "Now I'm learning how to dust the shelves."

"And how old are you?" I asked.

"Twelve," he blurted as if announcing a triumph of some sort.

"Twelve!" I thought to myself. "Why, he's just a boy."

Could I have been that young in 1958 when my grandfather handed me a pale green apron and put me to work in his grocery store? It was the first Saturday after my twelfth birthday, when Grandpa announced that I had come of age—at least in his mind. It would now be my job to run the store every Saturday. Grandpa would drive to the wholesale house and load up his Chevy with groceries for the week. Then he'd take care of "personal business" (playing poker with his cronies at the Elk's Club) while I held down the fort.

In my case, "holding down the fort" meant fetching items from behind the counter, scooping ice cream, slicing and wrapping baloney, pumping gas, totaling the sum on the back of a brown paper bag, counting out change, and bagging the purchases—all the while making sure nobody stole anything. All by myself.

After a ten-minute orientation period during which Grandpa taught me how to count back change and watch for thievery, he put on his suit coat, donned his gray fedora, walked out the back door, and left me in charge of everything he owned.

That's my training? I thought as I heard the Chevy pull away.

I soon learned that mom-and-pop grocery stores were no longer getting much business (big markets were taking over), so my job consisted largely of sitting in the back room and watching TV. That was, until the bell hanging just above the door announced a customer—jingle, jingle! Then I'd jump to my feet, push through the swinging door that separated the store from Grandpa's living quarters, step up to the counter, and ask, "May I help you?"

With time, all of that sitting around and waiting grew boring, so I invited my friends to visit me at the store. We'd play five-card draw in the back room. That was, until a customer would enter—jingle, jingle!

Then I'd break away from my buddies and impatiently wait on whoever had the nerve to disturb my poker game. About six months into the job, I became so tired of waiting on slow-moving customers that my friends and I decided it would be fun to play a trick on the worst offenders—kids who would show up with a two-cent pop bottle to trade for penny candy and then take *forever* making their choice.

So I invented a prank. I would crack open a can of chili powder, remove a plug from a hollow gumball, and fill the hollow with the red-hot powder. Then I would replace the plug and place the loaded candy onto the lip of the gumball machine that sat on the counter next to the till.

"Say, look at that!" I'd exclaim with a look of surprise as a kid walked up to the counter with a pop bottle. "Somebody forgot their gumball."

"I love that stuff," one of my friends would add.

The unsuspecting kid would look at the brightly colored sphere and then glance back at me for approval. I'd pause for effect and then add the *pièce de résistance*. "Go ahead, you can have it. Someone must have left it behind."

Immediately a hand would dart through the air, grab the candy, and stuff it into a welcoming mouth.

Then my friends and I would wait. First, the kid would roll the orb around in his or her mouth, tasting the scrumptious outer layer. Next, a small nibble. Then came the payoff—a big bite followed by a few rapid chews and eyes that would suddenly widen to full aperture. Next came a howl, followed by feet rushing through the door—jingle, jingle!—and ending with the kid leaping off the porch and spitting the fiery concoction onto the gravel.

"What's *wrong* with that gum?" the kid would ask with a look of betrayal.

We never answered, because my friends and I would be doubled over with laughter. It was just the kind of thing twelve-year-old boys find hilarious. It was also mean-spirited and wrong on many levels.

My buddies and I carried out this trick for a couple of Saturdays, until somebody ratted us out. My father lectured me, but I could tell from his repressed smile that he thought the whole thing was pretty funny. Mom chided me for falling in with a crowd of hardened delinquents.

Grandpa took a more reasonable approach. He asked me what I was thinking. This was hard to answer, because I was thinking that causing kids to believe that their mouth was on fire was hilarious—which made me sound demented.

Eventually, Grandpa ended his reproof with the classic guilt trip.

"I expected more of you."

Those five words were a shot to my heart. Then, to drive the point home, Grandpa banished my friends and docked me two Saturdays' wages.

From that day forward, I worked to regain my grandfather's trust. I scrubbed the shelves, washed windows, and sorted pop bottles for the entire eight-hour shift. I also treated every customer with respect. Especially the kids.

I tell this story because as I watch my own grandchildren grow older, I know they too will do childish things. And then when they're old enough to know better, they'll still do childish things. They're wired that way. Research reveals that some of the logical parts of an adolescent's brain don't fully develop until around age eighteen.

Fortunately, if adults follow my grandfather's lead and watch over their errant wards as their brains develop, correct them when necessary, and hold them accountable, they probably won't fall in with a den of thieves. And hopefully, when they take their first job and mess up as well, a wise boss will do the same.

At a time when the press takes every new crime statistic as evidence of an oncoming Armageddon, it's hard to maintain a proper sense of proportion. Not every drop of rain portends an oncoming storm, nor does every sighting of a locust signal a massive swarm just over the horizon.

More often than not, the rain stops after a light sprinkling, the locust continues solitarily down the path, and a boy in a pale green apron grows up.

SIX DOLLARS AN HOUR

///

Thug: You're gonna give us $10,000, or
we're gonna break both your legs.
Jack Benny: Does it have to be both?

THE JACK BENNY PROGRAM

On a generosity scale from one to ten—one meaning "painfully cheap" and ten meaning "delightfully generous"—my kids think I'm a one. For years I thought all the "You're Number One" cards, trophies, and plaques my children gave me on Father's Day celebrated my best-ness. It turns out it was code. They were mocking my cheapness. In fact, they think my entire generation is cheap.

Now, before you Gen Xers, Millennials, and other Post-Boomers join forces with my children in condemning my generation for being inordinately thrifty, take a walk in our slippers. See what life was like growing up as a teenager in the 60s. One look at a typical school day, and you might replace your contempt for my generation's penny-pinching with an appreciation for our financial conservatism. Stranger things have happened.

When I was in high school, I would get up every weekday morning and face the same question: Should I pack a lunch? My parents were unwilling to give me money to "throw away on fast food," so if I wanted a noon meal, I would have to make my own lunch—and it had to be sandwiches. This would have been perfectly fine were it not for the fact that in order to save money,

Mom generally purchased tongue, heart, liver, and other internal organs to be used as lunch meats.

So here was my typical school day: I would peer into the fridge and immediately reject tongue. Whenever I ate tongue, I couldn't figure out who was tasting whom. Heart and liver were also out of the question, because the mere sight of them freaked out my lunch mates. If I went so far as to take a bite of, say, boiled heart on raisin bread, it caused an epidemic of shiver-gags. I don't even want to talk about the scene a tripe sandwich could cause.

Later on, as lunchtime rolled around, I'd be famished and, for reasons you now understand, without a sandwich. This presented me with the second question of the day: Should I use the quarter my parents had given me to ride the bus home to purchase fast food? Or should I save my quarter for the bus and avert the hike home? If I sprang for fast food, my two bits would buy either a see-through milkshake or a tiny, pretend hamburger that contained no actual organic materials.

Given these options, I typically skipped lunch, but to no real advantage. At the end of the school day, I would again face the "eat vs. ride" decision. Only now, a bakery that sat next to the city bus stop made the choice even more difficult. It sold (and this was just plain cruel) twenty-five-cent cream puffs. Yum, cream puffs.

While waiting for the bus, I'd stare longingly through the bakery window at the delectable treats—fiercely gripping my quarter as if it were the key to Donald Trump's safe deposit box. Eventually, I would step out from under the bakery's awning to see how hard it was raining. If it wasn't raining too hard, and if the cream puffs looked particularly scrumptious, I would surrender my quarter, wolf down a cream puff, and walk home.

Oh yes, one more detail. I didn't merely walk home. I walked home while lugging a stack of textbooks. I completed this feat (as did all teenage boys in the 60s) by cocking my right arm unnaturally high and tucking my books into my armpit as if to say, "Look at me and my many muscles that can easily hold aloft these heavy books!" This ridiculous balancing act was extremely difficult to maintain and made me think twice about walking anywhere.

So, if it was raining hard and I had a lot of books to carry, I'd have to be a nitwit to give up my bus fare—which, I'm ashamed to admit, I did regularly because I adored cream puffs and possessed not a trace of willpower.

But not without consequences.

Once I had given into the allure of French pastry, I'd grudgingly hoist my books to their unnaturally high position and trudge a mile and a half up the hill to my house. Within a few minutes, a city bus would mockingly cruise by while the kids inside laughed at the sap lugging books up the hill in the rain. All of this took place because I couldn't stand tasting a sandwich only to have it return the favor.

Now, keep in mind, this drama was about a quarter. Two bits. Twenty-five cents. You can only imagine what it took for me to spend a lot of money. I did earn money through various jobs, but every cent of that went to buying clothes. When it came to saving for frills, I had to skip lunch and walk home—sans the high-octane fuel of French pastry—often for days on end. For instance, during my senior year when I elected to go to the prom, for several months I hungrily walked home in the rain, lugging my books like a stevedore. And while I did, here's what I'd be thinking:

Let's see, my date wants a purple flower to match her dress—five bucks (or twenty quarters). The prom tickets cost four dollars (sixteen quarters). Photos are another four. Dinner—please don't let her order steak!—fifteen bucks (a whopping sixty quarters). Plus there's the tuxedo and . . .

I hadn't thought about that prom until one day thirty years later when my mother produced a piece of paper she had set aside the day after the dance. It was an itemized list I'd made of what I had spent. At the bottom of the list I had calculated the total dollar figure and divided it by the number of hours the date had lasted—revealing that the prom had cost me six dollars an hour.

I know, I know. The fact that I calculated how much the prom cost per hour brands me a hopeless cheapskate. Nevertheless, having just walked in my slippers, I hope you now understand my cautious ways. You know that as a young man I rarely had any money or a chance to get any. That is, unless I walked a mile and a half uphill in the rain carrying a stack of books jammed under my armpit.

So, dear friends, forgive me my frugality. Show patience as I—and others from my generation—ask the restaurant cashier for change for a quarter and then return to the table to leave an exact 15 percent tip. Smile knowingly when we refuse to turn on the air conditioning, buy discounted label-less cans, and wash and reuse the plasticware that comes with fast food. Take pity on us old codgers who, on occasion, can appear to be a tad cheap.

We have our reasons.

A SECOND FIRST TIME

///

"He who can no longer pause to wonder and stand rapt
in awe, is as good as dead; his eyes are closed."

ALBERT EINSTEIN

I grew up in a one-bedroom house at the end of a long dirt road in
the middle of the forest. Should you visit our place, you'd expect
to find Thoreau seated in a corner, poised over a manuscript and
mumbling about the simple life. In keeping with this image, in
my early years our home had no radio, no TV (not until my third-
grade year), and most certainly no computer. To say I lived an
insulated childhood would be an understatement.

I remember the day when all of this changed. Our neighbor,
Wilson Cowslip, asked my mother if it would be okay to take me
to the county fair with his son Jimmy—my friend and first-grade
classmate. I had no idea what a county fair was, but given my circumstances, I would have gone along just to ride in Mr. Cowslip's
'43 Chevy.

After we parked and walked up to the fairgrounds, we happened
upon a snack stand. I couldn't believe what I saw. The tiny shed
contained foods and confections I had never imagined. I immediately settled on a magical wad of cotton candy. It was the perfect
food—sugar, plus more sugar. Where had they been hiding this
stuff?

From the snack stand, the three of us walked to the midway,
where I learned that you could win terrific prizes such as stuffed

poodles, silver horse figurines, and chalk Popeye statues. After throwing baseballs at bottles so long and poorly that the worker operating the concession took pity on me, I won a stuffed monkey that I thought was so wonderful I wouldn't let go of it for two days.

Then came the real animals. The first structure we entered housed pedigreed rabbits, guinea pigs, and pigeons. Each animal was more bizarre and beautiful than the previous. Huge fuzzy ears, radiant tail feathers, fur so thick it covered the animal's eyes— could there be anything more adorable? Some of the pigeons, I learned, if released into the air, would do somersaults. Imagine— acrobatic birds!

Next came the show animals. There was a bull large enough to carry our entire house on its back. Nearby we encountered gloriously colored chickens that looked as if they had just escaped from a Disney cartoon. At one point, I came across a steer whose horns were so sharp and wide, I stood frozen on the spot. I couldn't move. Where had they been hiding these animals before I visited the fair? Certainly nowhere near our house on 25th Street.

When I arrived home that evening, I nearly dislocated my arms, so wild were my gesticulations as I described to my mom and dad the wonders I had seen for the very first time. That day, I must have experienced more than a hundred "first times."

But the wonder eventually faded. With time and repeated exposure, the fascinating became the routine until the routine eventually wilted into the boring. Consequently, twenty years later when the local county fair was promoted on TV, I wasn't the least bit interested in visiting the dreary old fairgrounds—that was, until my boys begged me to take them. I reluctantly agreed.

Then something marvelous transpired. When the three of us arrived at the fair, the worn-out place was made new to me through the eyes of my boys. It was their first time. Even though they had lived a far more diverse life than I had on 25th Street, they were still excited by the sounds, smells, and sights of the fair.

My sons reveled as they stood in the shadows of the enormous animals. And so did I. They purchased massive turkey drumsticks and walked around chewing on them like pirates, shouting, "Arrrg!" And so did I. Then came the *coup de grâce*. Each of us bought a mystery box at the rock-house display, poured out the sand, and discovered our very own thunder egg—complete with accompanying quartz crystals. Now my sons weren't merely pirates, they were treasure-toting pirates! And so was I.

Later that day, as I sat at home basking in the glow of a successful outing, I became aware of something I had experienced before, but now I had a name for it. While it was true that I would never have the same first-time experience I'd had years earlier by simply returning to the fair (or something equally grand)—if my children accompanied me and experienced the event for *their* first time, I could enjoy a second first time through their eyes.

We do such things all the time. We take a friend to a play we've already seen, not simply to view the play again, but to watch our friend and borrow a bit of his or her first-time reaction. When we do, we enjoy a second first time.

It took another twenty years for researchers to fully understand this particular phenomenon. As it turns out, human brains are filled with what are known as mirror neurons. When others are experiencing an emotional event, our mirror neurons are set into action, and when they are, we don't merely feel sympathetic toward others—it's as if the experience is actually happening to us. Mirror neurons allow us the glorious luxury of experiencing a second first time.

I know this sounds strange, but I can be a bit purposeful when it comes to exploiting my own mirror neurons. Aware of the power of these tiny cells, I look for chances to hitchhike off the emotions of the uninitiated. At the age of sixty-seven, I volunteer my time by teaching an MBA class where newcomers help remind me of why I love the field. I serve as a mentor at work by meeting once a week with young employees and discussing the history of our books and products. Oh yes, and with regard to my grandchildren,

A SECOND FIRST TIME
53

I can't wait to take them to new sights and experiences where I can enjoy third first times.

As a parting comment, I'll concede that not all first-time experiences fade and can only be revived by a second first time. We have titanium-like experiences that don't wear, rust, or weaken with use. In fact, they can be experienced over and over and never lose their luster.

I was reminded of this fact yesterday when my daughter shared the following experience. As she watched her five-year-old son, Tommy, play with action figures, complete with cute sound effects, she turned to him and said, "I love you, Tommy." He looked up at her, smiled, and responded, "I know, Mommy." Then, after thinking about it for a moment, he looked up again and said, "But you can keep telling me."

Some things just never get old.

～

YOU DON'T BELONG!

//

"I refuse to join any club that would
have me as a member."

GROUCHO MARX

I couldn't believe my good fortune. Preston Coventry, one of the more popular kids in the ninth grade, had invited me to the grand opening of his neighborhood association's swimming pool. When the appointed day arrived, I hiked across town to the posh facility where I was greeted by a tall fence and a stern guard. After I waited a couple of minutes, Preston approached the gate, gave a quick nod, the guard pushed a button, and I was granted entrance.

Preston and I spent the entire day playing water games and chasing girls with squirt guns. It was perfectly wonderful. I had no idea that such a life even existed. But then my thoughts turned to the long walk home, so I changed clothes and headed toward the exit. As the gate shut behind me, I turned around. Then I grabbed two of the metal bars, stuck my head between them, and smiled at Preston. (I was lobbying for an invitation to return.) Preston glanced back at me and abruptly stated, "You can't come back."

"What?" I managed to ask.

"You're not allowed to return," Preston repeated. "You don't belong."

"What do you mean I don't belong?" I asked.

"You don't belong to the association. You're a guest and are allowed only one visit a year. You've already had your turn."

I managed a feeble "thank you," extracted my head from the gate, and walked home. With each step, the words *You don't belong* rang painfully in my head. Then it hit me. Up until that moment my friends and I had largely played in empty fields and open waterways. All of it was free, so we were all equal. Now there was a pool, a fence, a gate, a guard, and rules. The "haves" played gleefully on one side while I trudged down the long dirt road that snaked into the heart of the valley of the "have-nots."

You might think this event turned me into an avid socialist, but it didn't. I didn't fault the wealthy for locking the gate. Who could blame them? But it did put a question into my fourteen-year-old brain: Where *did* I belong? I pondered that question for quite some time.

Two decades passed, until I eventually decided I belonged at a university. At least, a part of me did. So in 1980, when I finished graduate school, I accepted a faculty position. At last, I had found a place where I belonged.

Before I gave my first lecture, I decided that it was time to take precautions. Having been raised by parents who had lived through the Great Depression and who spoke often of its soon-to-arrive sequel, I began the semiparanoid task of transforming my entire backyard into a massive vegetable garden. Let the Great Debacle arrive—I'd have zucchini! So when the first day of the semester rolled around, instead of poring over my lecture notes as most faculty members did, I borrowed a truck from my neighbor and hauled pig manure to mix with my garden's depleted soil.

All morning long I hauled loads of compost from a nearby pig farm and flung the disgusting muck onto my garden bed. Then I frantically changed my clothes and hustled to campus to attend my very first faculty meeting. I couldn't believe it. I—the poor kid who lived down the long dirt road—would be part of a faculty meeting in which acclaimed educator Stephen R. Covey was scheduled to lead the discussion. He had been developing ideas about several key habits and was eager to discuss them with the rest of us.

As Dr. Covey launched into his presentation, I couldn't help but notice a horrible stench in the room. Soon everyone started to squint, cough, and look for the source of the smell. Then I noticed my socks. Uh oh. When I changed from my farm clothes into my sports coat and slacks, I had neglected to change my manure-tainted socks, which were now emitting a repugnant odor.

It wasn't long until my colleagues began to eyeball me—the apparent source of the smell. I fessed up. I told them about my garden, its depleted soil, the pig manure, and my socks. After a moment's reflection, everyone laughed, I slid over to a far corner of the room, Steve moved on to turning endings into beginnings, and I thanked my lucky stars for having escaped untarnished.

But then Preston Coventry's jarring voice hit me. The words *You don't belong!* reverberated through my insecure soul. One look at the scholars in the room, and I was certain that none of them had ever flung pig manure and then carried the stench to a faculty meeting. These folks were polished and sophisticated. They had lovely homes, pools (probably locked), and pedigrees. They belonged. I didn't. It took only a glance to see that.

Later that evening while visiting with my mother, I told her about the stinky-sock debacle and admitted that I didn't believe I belonged at a university. She wouldn't have it.

"The idea of *belonging* to anything is just plain silly," Mom argued. "Sure, clubs set rules about who they let in, but in things that matter, belonging is irrelevant. It's not how you measure up to others' standards that matters; it's how you feel about yourself—and that comes from being comfortable with what you do."

"Yeah, but look what I've *done*," I responded. "I went to a faculty meeting reeking of pig manure. Then to make matters worse, I admitted to the mistake in public."

"Precisely," my mother said. "And that makes you unassuming, not unworthy."

"No, that makes me a hick, and a stupid one to boot."

I continued to put up a fuss, but eventually decided that I would follow Mom's advice and work on being satisfied with what I had done and who I had become, rather than where others thought I belonged—or worse still, where I thought they thought I belonged.

For the most part, this strategy has served me well, but I'd be lying if I said I'm always comfortable in my skin. There are days when I feel as if I'm that kid standing outside that swimming pool, desperately gripping the bars and peering into a world that doesn't want me. And then on those odd occasions when I happen to gain entry, I'm haunted by the feeling that I'm going to be asked to leave.

But then I think of the pig manure and the wonderful crops it nurtured. It helped grow a cabbage so large it didn't fit into a bushel basket. The beets tasted like candy. My kids still talk about the sweet corn. It was heavenly.

But best of all, the pig droppings came with a lesson. If you want to be content in life, you have to be able to fling manure without looking over your shoulder to see who approves. If you can't do that, life is a long, lonely stretch. People will continue to suggest that you don't belong, and you'll believe them. So give up the silly notion of belonging, and think of who you are and the wonderful things you do. That's where you'll find satisfaction.

Oh yes, and don't forget to change your socks.

LIFE LESSONS

THINGS ARE GOING TO BE OKAY

///////////////////////////////////

"I had a terrible education. I attended a school
for emotionally disturbed teachers."

WOODY ALLEN

I didn't learn much in elementary school. No knock on the teachers. The neighborhood surrounding my school was peppered
with deadbeats who treated new ideas like an invading virus. The
administration's goal wasn't so much about teaching as it was
about keeping kids out of juvie.

Now, taking a hiatus from learning during the entire Eisen-
hower administration would have been of little consequence were
it not for the fact that when I eventually moved on to junior high,
I was thrown in with a group of elite seventh-graders. As part of a
secret school experiment, these students had been handpicked for
excellent academic preparation. Everyone, that was, save me—I
was the token poor kid.

Imagine that it's the first day of class at your new junior high
school. Halfway through your homeroom class, you discover that
every single student (except for you) had been registered at a private school across town since they were embryos. Then, starting
at age five, and for the next six years, they'd been showered with
tutors and special programs.

I had experienced no such preparation. Consequently, on the first day of class when Mr. Kavossi barked, "Diagram this sentence!" I knew I was in trouble.

"Is that a predicate nominative or a predicate adjective?" Aaron Rand inquired.

"Do you want us to follow the standard protocol or the Helsinki Variation?" Kathy Harper asked.

"So *that's* what a sentence looks like," I quietly muttered.

And thus went my entire precollege education. Every single day of school I was reminded how ill prepared and utterly stupid I was by classmates who were given memberships to Mensa for their fourth birthdays.

Years passed, until going to college finally threw me in with a more normal crowd. With practice, I was able to come up with the occasional right answer. And then, just when I arrived at the point where I figured I wasn't a total moron, I was admitted to a *really* challenging graduate school. Once again, I found myself surrounded by folks who had been registered for exclusive private schools since they were embryos—only, they'd been embryos with money.

"How might you use the overjustification hypothesis to explain this phenomenon?" a fellow grad student asked me.

"Is that the standard version or the Helsinki Variation?" another student chimed in.

Oh boy.

And so went another three years of humiliation until one day, totally by accident, I learned what it felt like to have people admire me rather than snicker at my very appearance. I experienced something, I now contend, everyone should encounter at least once before he or she dies.

In my case, my brush with respect came in late 1979, just about the time my academic self-confidence was hitting its nadir. Our grad-school social coordinator decided to hold small-group parties at faculty members' homes scattered in and around Palo Alto. The party you were to attend was based on the first letter of your surname. So we were supposed to wear costumes that represented P things.

What P things? I wondered. Then it struck me! My wife would go to the P-party as a patient (she'd have psoriasis and pneumonia), and I'd be her physician. The medical student living in the apartment next door lent me latex gloves, a stethoscope, and a complete set of *purple* scrubs—pants, boots, jacket, and hat.

This particular party took place long before the advent of GPS equipment or mobile phones, so when Louise and I became lost on the way, I pulled up to a restaurant and ran in the front door. I figured I could use the pay phone to call our hosts and ask for directions. Unfortunately, I didn't have change for the phone, and there was a line at the cash register. This wasn't going well.

And then it hit me. I didn't have to wait in any stinking line. I was a doctor!

"I need change for the pay phone!" I blurted to the restaurant patrons politely standing in line.

Everyone turned and stared at me.

"And I need it NOW!"

The sea of customers parted as I hustled my way to the counter while the hostess frantically fished out a dime.

Okay, maybe I hadn't thought this through. I was now on the pay phone asking the P-party host for directions, and I had to make the call sound like a medical emergency. After all, I had just crashed the line.

"Don't worry," I blurted, "I'll have the heart there in a few minutes."

The ruse worked. Nobody questioned me. Never mind the fact that I had put on rubber gloves *miles away* from what apparently was going to be a home-style heart transplant. Hey, I was a physician—delivering a heart. And did I mention I was wearing purple scrubs?

I'll never forget the looks of admiration afforded me by the restaurant patrons I had just hoodwinked. It was wonderful. Then I turned on my heel, smiled, and shouted:

"Thanks, folks, you just helped save a life!"

With these parting words, I exited the room with a confident flair I've been unable to duplicate since. I think one of my eyeteeth actually sparkled.

Of course, the heady feeling I enjoyed that day was unearned and short-lived, but I did get a big laugh later that evening when I told my P-party grad-school friends what happened. We were each caught halfway between being a trainee and being a "somebody"—or at least a graduate—and were chomping at the bit. We wanted our turn at the front of the class. We wanted the looks of admiration.

And while I can't in good conscience recommend that anyone don surgery garb and crash lines to get a feel for absolute adoration, I can say that if you stick to your books, classes, and work assignments, the day will come when you will be the knowing one. You're not likely to be the *all*-knowing one (that's reserved for those Mensa folks), but someday you'll be an expert of sorts and it will be well worth the effort.

I'll never forget the day I finally stood in front of a class as an assistant professor. Thirty eager students were all looking at me. That's right, me, the kid who couldn't diagram a sentence. When I spoke, they listened. Some even took notes. And, of course, some asked questions.

"Is that explanation based on social cognitive theory?" a student from the back row inquired.

"Are you referring to the standard version or the Helsinki Variation?" I responded.

Things were going to be okay.

THE SKY'S THE LIMIT

///

"The expectations of life depend upon diligence;
the mechanic that would perfect his work
must first sharpen his tools."

CONFUCIUS

M y report card always caused a ruckus at my home. My eighth-grade midterm report was no exception. I thought Mom was going to choke when she saw the five Cs and one B. Now don't get me wrong, she wasn't upset with the Cs. I was typically a C student back in those days. It was the B in math that got her goat. I had always earned an A in math. My math scores were her only hope for bragging rights, and she wasn't about to let them drop without a fight.

"How do you explain this B?" Mom asked.

Not knowing what to say, I blurted out the first thing that came to my mind: "Miss Needlebom, my math teacher, is mean. I don't dare ask questions, because if you raise your hand she bites it off."

Anxious to right the wrong, Mom set an appointment to meet the very next day with Mr. Howard, the principal. I shuddered at the thought of my mother talking with the one man who knew so much about what I actually did at school. Nothing good could come from such an encounter.

Mom returned from the appointment with an odd look on her face. Perhaps the conference hadn't gone so poorly after all. Maybe Mr. Howard had admitted to the fact that Miss Needlebom was an inept and cruel teacher, and I was now off the hook. Anything's possible, right?

Mom was the first to speak. "It turns out Miss Needlebom suffers from the effects of polio. She's always in pain, and that's why she's so grumpy."

Just my luck. I finally got the goods on one of my junior high school's finest purveyors of emotional abuse and she trumped my complaint with polio.

"Now, don't get me wrong," Mom continued. "Mr. Howard said he'd speak to Miss Needlebom about being more responsive to your questions, and I'm sure that'll help. But there's more," Mom continued. "As I was leaving the principal's office, Mr. Howard made a comment that caught me by surprise."

What could he have said? Was it the fact that Gary Lupino and I had snuck into the gym during lunch and used the climbing ropes as Tarzan swings? Was it that I had thrown Jeff Kilgore's metal-shop project into the forge, cranked up the billows, and melted it?

"Mr. Howard said that you should be getting better grades—mostly As," Mom explained. "He checked into the achievement tests you've taken over the years, and he thinks you have the potential to be on the honor roll."

"You're kidding," I said in genuine disbelief.

"No, those were his exact words. You should be getting good grades."

And with those six words, my life changed forever. According to an official educator who had looked into my "test scores" (whatever that meant), I should be able to earn good grades. More than that, I was *expected* to do so. Mom immediately bought into the news, whereas I suspected that Mr. Howard had made the whole thing up to get me to pay attention in class, do homework, and otherwise become a nerd.

Then Mr. Howard drove the final nail into my coffin of skylarking and tomfoolery. He not only talked of my potential, but he also suggested to my mom that I wouldn't earn those good grades if I continued to leave my books in my locker. In fact, he recommended that I sit down at home for two hours every evening and study.

It had to be a joke. Mom didn't think so. From that moment on, I did two hours of homework every night. As you might imagine, going from doing not a lick of homework to completing one hundred and twenty minutes of genuine study every night dramatically changed my grades, my self-image, and eventually my life. All of this changed because of raised expectations and the behavior that followed.

I'm not the only one who has suffered from the effects of anemic expectations. You see it all the time. A couple of nights ago, an in-law told me that he was born with a bad temper, so there was nothing he could do about his violent, verbal outbursts. It was in his genes.

"I'm a genetic victim," he actually said aloud. He thought it was a legitimate alibi. I saw it differently. With his crippling statement regarding his limited expectations, I heard a thousand doors slam shut.

I point out the power of expectations—to both inspire and repress—at a time when I'm not sure we could expect less from our students, and in many cases, from our employees. Granted, you can always find overscheduled students and overworked employees, but by and large, we expect little of both. In an employee survey my partners and I once conducted, forty percent of those polled suggested that they did not do one ounce of work more than what was required to keep them from getting fired. To suggest that they're underachieving is a gross understatement.

At school, it's often no better. Across three decades, I've taught second-year graduate students a course that requires them to write papers that call for both creative writing and critical thought. Many complain that it's the first paper they've been required to write in their entire college experience. Until that point, they have attended classes, memorized material, and taken tests where they mostly filled in bubble boxes. Plus, they have hidden in large classes where they rarely, if ever, had to make a comment. As a result, many graduate from college without ever having made either verbal or written arguments. Nor do they expect to do so.

I mentioned the importance of setting high expectations to a colleague of mine, and he quickly jumped in with the notion that children need to be affirmed at school and at home. When I asked him for details, he insisted that the affirmation needed to be about each child's general worth as a human being—each is a good person.

Here's where it gets tricky. It turns out that if you tell kids that they're good (in a general sense), they know that they just had a bad thought or just did a bad thing and don't see themselves as good. They see you as naïve. With non-specific praise, you're unlikely to increase others' self-esteem and are simultaneously doing damage to your own credibility.

So, when setting high expectations, focus on specific behaviors or skills rather than offering generic affirmation. Then build in the elements of deliberate practice and helpful coaching, and the expectations eventually become reality.

Of one thing I am certain. I wouldn't have become a better student if my mother hadn't talked to Mr. Howard. He helped me change my expectations with six simple words—"He should be getting good grades." Then he put me to work.

So, as you interact with friends, family, and colleagues, bless them by helping them raise their expectations of their own performance. Maybe six words won't turn their lives around, but if you make it a routine practice to set higher standards and then help people achieve them, the sky's the limit. In fact, you might even go beyond the sky.

WILD DOGS AND CARD CATALOGS: AN ODE TO THE CLOUD

//

"Research is what I'm doing when I
don't know what I'm doing."

WERNHER VON BRAUN

It was the wish of Bellingham School District No. 501 that, starting in the seventh grade, each student write a weekly theme and an annual term paper—and continue this practice throughout all of his or her junior high and high school years. Themes were easy. I would sit down and write whatever cockamamie idea came to mind, turn it in, and then have it torn apart by college English majors who graded my work with a red pencil and hatchet.

We kids weren't taught much about how to actually write. In fact, I don't remember being taught *anything* about writing. The theory was to throw young writers in the water and see if they learn to avoid torturing a metaphor. In any case, every week, I wrote a paper that would come back marked with terms such as AWK, ¶, and DANG MOD.

This confidence-killing technique was small potatoes compared to the esteem-crushing, soul-sucking damage caused by the annual term paper. Unlike themes, term papers required library research from original sources. That meant I had to walk a mile to my grandfather's grocery store and buy three-by-five note cards.

"Poe, Twain—and I believe the Bard himself—used three-by-five cards," my seventh-grade English teacher, Mr. Lewis, explained. "It's how you organize your thoughts."

Required cards in hand, I walked another full mile and a half to the city library to start my research. And yes, I did have to fight off wild dogs along the way. It was the fifties, and wild dogs roamed the countryside. No kidding.

Once I arrived at the library, I milled about looking confused until Mrs. Huffington, the reference librarian, asked me if I needed help. This was, of course, said in a tone that indicated needing help was a sign of being hopelessly dim-witted. I told her about my upcoming term paper, explaining that I had narrowed my subject matter from a treatise on the universe to twelve pages about the planets.

Mrs. Huffington sneered at my topic, which she said was "grossly unfocused," took me to a three-mile-long card catalog, and then stood me in front of the P drawers. I chuckled at the sound of the expression "P drawers" while thumbing my way through an endless list of references about planets. Eventually, I picked a reference, recorded the code required to find it, and headed to the stacks.

After a long and dispiriting search, I came to a group of journals that sported numbers, letters, and secret symbols similar to the code I had written, only to discover that the edition I wanted wasn't on the shelf. So I hiked back to the sea of boxes, selected another reference, wandered the stacks, found the journal, turned to the section that had the information about planets, and— *voilà*—discovered that the pages I needed had been ripped out! This heinous act had surely been perpetrated by a previous student who didn't want to go to the trouble of writing down the information on his three-by-five cards. And obviously the student couldn't photo copy the pages, because the copy machines you can now find in every library nook and cranny *hadn't yet been invented.*

By now it was growing late, so I exited the library and started down the road that would take me the two-and-a-half miles home—without a single piece of information for my term paper.

It only got worse. Between slogs to the library, I had to read extremely complicated material about the planets—including Saturn, Neptune, Pluto, Mickey, and Dopey. (I was tempted to work this line into my term paper but came to my senses.) I also had to learn about the proper use of Latin footnote terms such as *op. cit.* and *ibid.* in preparation for the imminent resurgence of the Roman Empire.

Then came the monumental job of typing the paper on our family's manual Remington portable typewriter. And, heaven forbid I made a mistake, erasing typos with a steel-belted, paper-shredding Eberhard Faber eraser. I made so many mistakes and attempted so many corrections that my final product was a real dog's breakfast. It was so trashed that if you held it up to the light, it looked like a papyrus manuscript—had ancient scholars used an Aramaic Remington portable.

After feverishly working on my project for several weeks, I submitted it and eagerly awaited my grade. I had worked hard and was proud of my final document. I shouldn't have been. It came back covered with red marks of all sorts—and the grade C- over a D+.

"Look at this wonderful paper," Mr. Lewis exclaimed as he held up Sally Welch's glorious effort. My classmate Sally's mother had typed Sally's term paper on a fancy electric machine and it had zero typos. Plus, her parents had done most of the research and writing, earning Sally an A+ over an A+. But that didn't stop Sally from smiling broadly as Mr. Lewis heaped on the praise. She clearly was bound for glory, whereas I, the C- over D+ student, would probably end up in the food services industry as my school guidance counselor had suggested earlier that year. No lie.

At this point, you may think I'm about to launch into a rant about questionable teaching methods and egregious inequities. Not so. I'm simply trying to provide background material, particularly for people under the age of forty, for the thanks I'm about to offer.

"What thanks?" you ask. I recently spoke to a group of Google executives, but before I started into my assigned topic, I offered my heartfelt appreciation for their work, as well as the work of other search-engine designers.

I had just completed an entire book, chock-full of citations from original material, and in so doing, was not once attacked by a dog. I never had to hike in the pouring rain only to discover that the reference book I sought was missing. I never pulled a journal down from the shelf only to have key pages ripped out. Instead, I cheerfully scooted my computer mouse here and there, occasionally twitched my index finger, and magically uncovered material that, years earlier, would have taken days to find.

I now have the entire Library of Congress, along with just about anything anybody who ever had a thought has had to say, at my fingertips. Thank you, search-engine inventors, code writers, data scanners, and people who vacuum and do the plumbing for The Cloud. Thank you for turning our world into a place where information is as available and cheap as air itself.

I know, we're not always sure what to *do* with all the information that silently beams into our space in giga, tera, and super-giga–tera bundles. Nevertheless, it's time to offer a "good-on-ya" to everyone out there who has made finding what used to be largely unattainable a mere click away.

My guess is that my grandkids will never have a clue how hard it used to be to research and write a term paper—and I'm fine with that. But one thing is for certain. As they put together their papers, they won't be chased by dogs.

WILD MUSHROOMS

//

"Papa put his hand on my shoulder and said,
'Remember, my son, if you ever need a helping
hand, you'll find one at the end of your arm.'"

SAM LEVENSON

'm not sure exactly how old I was when my mom taught me how
to find wild mushrooms. I know she held my hand as we walked
into the woods that day. I can still feel the warm touch of her fingers. That would put me at around seven years of age. Any older
than that and I would have learned it was no longer "cool" to hold
hands with my mom. Pity.

No matter my exact age, it was springtime that day, and if you
knew where to search for them, you could find delicious mushrooms growing in the woods behind our home. But it wouldn't
be easy. After trekking through the woods for an hour, Mom
dropped five mushrooms into our brown paper bag. I had found
one. We eagerly took our bounty home, where Mom fried six
golden-brown morels and popped them into an omelet. This ritual
went on for a couple of weeks—the two of us searching hand-in-
hand and eventually returning with a half dozen or so mushrooms.

Then, one Saturday morning, my world changed. Driven by
some genetic, time-released code hidden deep inside my cells, I
sprang out of bed, grabbed a bag, and went in search of edible
fungi *on my own*. For reasons I'll never understand, the hunter–
gatherer inside me had been activated.

I still remember how frightened I was as I walked into the thick, dark woods behind our home. I hadn't actually seen any of the "wild things" that lived there. But I certainly had heard their occasional growls and trembled at the sight of their tracks. Nevertheless, my desire to prove my mettle outweighed my fears. It was my time to step up to the table. It was my time to provide for the table. So, I plunged into the darkness, eyes pinned to the forest floor—dead set on becoming a provider.

It was hard work finding mushrooms that day. The woods were damp; blackberry vines scratched my arms, cockleburs stuck to my socks, and stinging nettles rubbed against my neck and ankles—leaving behind tiny mountain ranges of welts. All the while, the mushrooms hid.

After more than an hour of fruitless (or fungi-less?) searching, and just before I trudged home in utter defeat, I stumbled into a small, dank hollow that offered the first mushroom of the day. As I knelt down to gather it up, there, next to it, I saw another—and then another.

Startled by the find, I jumped to my feet and gave my eyes a second to adjust; there, peeking their heads through the loam, were dozens of edible delights. I'll never forget that glorious moment. On my first solo attempt, I had stumbled on the mother lode of mushrooms. Like a modern-day conqueror, I would soon be returning home with the spoils—a paper bag filled to the top with *Morchella esculenta*.

I burst through the front door—scratched, nettle-stung, and wet—and Mom beamed with delight when she saw what I was carrying. My brother gave me an enthusiastic thumbs-up. Dad slapped me on the back, carefully inspected my bounty, washed it, and fried the lot in butter. Then the four of us sat down at the family table and feasted on a delicious breakfast that I, a seven-year-old boy, had gathered all by myself.

In most cultures, it's common for young people to go through a formal rite of passage into manhood. Some do so at church, others during a tribal ceremony, still others do it the first time their Dad tosses them the keys to the car.

But not with me. I was only seven years old the day I brought home those mushrooms—about half the number of years most people think it takes to spring into manhood. Yet I'm pretty sure I made the leap right then and there. As everyone could plainly see, I had stepped up from being merely a consumer to being a provider.

And provide I did. From mushroom gathering I graduated to berry picking, clam digging, and fishing. We were poor during my childhood years, but we ate well. Imagine a dinner comprised of wild mushrooms, butter clams, trout, and hot blackberry pie. It's the kind of fare they serve at fancy restaurants nowadays. It's the "in" thing to eat. For us, it was the free thing to eat. For me, it was my chance to provide.

I hadn't thought about this part of my life until recently, when two of my granddaughters invited me to a fashion show at the local grade school. At age nine, the two of them had taken a sewing class from one of our neighbors, and now they were going to model the blouse and skirt each of them had made. As each paraded around the cafeteria, I nearly burst with pride. Imagine that. Making their own clothes—and in only the fourth grade! Later that evening as we talked, the two girls stood confidently, wrapped in clothes of their own making.

As I looked closely into their eyes, I could tell that both girls had changed. I had seen them perform ballet, gymnastics, cheerleading, piano, violin—you name it, they had taken the lessons and performed at the recitals. But this was different. They were different.

Most of the lessons kids take are about performing for an audience and then basking in the applause that follows. While I believe in such training and the skills, confidence, and discipline it develops, it's not the same as producing something the family can use. It's not the same as adding to the country's gross national product.

It's not the same as picking mushrooms, digging clams, or sewing your own clothes. Accomplish that, and you become a provider.

Not to put too fine a point on this, but I do believe the difference between performing and providing, although subtle, is substantial. Praising a kid for completing a pirouette is one thing. Praising a child for bringing home food teaches the importance of not only accomplishment, but also the importance of offering service.

My son-in-law, Bruce, understands this point all too well. On his twelfth birthday, his father asked him to help earn money for their family by tending sheep every day before and after school. His dad invested in a flock, and for four years Bruce faithfully carried out his job of tending, mucking, shearing, and the like until he returned home from school one day to discover his family flock was gone.

"Where are they?" Bruce asked his father.

"Oh, we don't need the sheep anymore," his father explained. "Actually, we never really needed them. I just wanted you to learn how to work."

You have to love that story. Bruce's father wanted to help give his son the sense of joy and accomplishment that comes with being a provider. Unlike my home on Bellingham Bay, you couldn't find mushrooms, clams, oysters, or salmon near Bruce's home in the suburbs just outside Salt Lake City.

But you could find sheep.

WHAT DO YOU REALLY WANT?

//

"Things which matter most must never be at
the mercy of things which matter least."

JOHANN WOLFGANG VON GOETHE

If you were to visit our home, there are a couple of things you might have trouble reconciling. The potted plants leading up to our front door are shabby, disheveled, and imbalanced, whereas the carpets inside are so clean you could perform surgery on them. Why the inconsistency?

It all started some twenty years ago while I was observing a plant manager give a speech. It was a tough time for the company, and she was explaining in an all-hands meeting why they were cutting back on the budget. She argued that everyone was going to have to sacrifice.

When the executive eventually called for questions, there was a long, awkward pause. Finally, an employee standing in the back raised his hand. His comments shook the room. "If money is so tight," the nervous fellow remarked, "then why are you building a second office across town for yourself? And I hear that it's costing tens of thousands of dollars. How can you justify that?"

This was one of those tense moments we've all experienced at work. Everyone quickly sucked in their breath as they waited for the executive to blow a gasket and humiliate the person who asked the imprudent question. After all, the guy had just called the boss a hypocrite in front of the entire company. Clearly, he would pay. Sure enough, the boss turned dark red while the muscles in her face tightened.

But then the executive caught herself. She took a deep breath, relaxed, smiled, and thanked the person for the question. She explained the business reason behind the decision and said she was unaware of the actual budget, but if it was indeed as high as just reported, she would make sure to take corrective action. This conversation continued until everyone seemed satisfied with what was going on, and the meeting ended on a positive note.

As we walked back to her office, I asked the executive how she was able to keep from losing her temper when an employee had called her a hypocrite. She explained that at first she was upset. The question had come across as a cheap shot. But then she said something that I've never forgotten. She explained, "As I was becoming angry, I asked myself what I really wanted. Did I want to humiliate this guy in front of the crowd? My emotions cried for this, but it's not what I really wanted. I wanted everyone to buy into the notion that times were indeed tough and that we needed to be financially responsible. If there were rumors floating around that had to be answered before people would believe the message, then I needed to hear them. The truth is, I needed him to ask the very question he asked. So I thanked him, and I meant it. It was the best thing that could have happened."

When you're in the middle of a heated discussion, asking what you really want turns out to be one of the most important questions you can pose to yourself. If you don't ask it, and your emotions take over, there's a good chance you'll move from wanting to make the best choice to wanting to discredit or even humiliate the other person.

With this concept in mind, let's return to my home and reveal how my flowers got so tattered, while the carpet became so clean.

Is this disparity evidence that I'm an obsessive-compulsive with traces of schizophrenia? Or is something else going on?

Here's the answer. When my mother passed away a few years back, my father moved in with us. He's a wonderful fellow, always upbeat and trying to help out despite the fact that he is in his late eighties and mostly blind. That first spring, just after he moved in, I started to fill our front flower pots and planters with the perennials I'd purchased. Dad shuffled up next to me, gloves in hand, ready to help.

It turned out to be a tough job—to include Dad, that is. He could barely see, so when I asked him to water after I put the plants in the soil, he harmed the delicate flowers. Either he knocked off the blooms with the hose or he flushed away the soil with too much water pressure. He then hinted that watering the plants would now be his daily job. When I suggested that I could do it, he looked disappointed and said that he really wanted to pitch in.

It's not easy growing old. Giving away your life's possessions as you move from a house to an apartment to a single room can't be fun. Watching your body give out one part at a time must be frightening. And now, as he stood there with hose nozzle in hand, Dad faced the prospect of no longer contributing to the family.

At first, I told Dad not to worry about watering: I'd do it. I took pride in my flower beds and pots. Each summer, people would compliment our lovely flowers. My wife and oldest son, having watched Dad at work, sidled up next to me and suggested that I couldn't let him help with the flowers. It would be a disaster.

As I talked with Dad, he continued to plead his case. He'd be really careful, and watering would give him something to do. We had been struggling with how to fill his days. Right?

And then it hit me—the words of the executive echoed in my head. What did I really want? Obviously, I wanted Dad to be happy. But then again, I also wanted the plants to look good. Maybe I could find another job for him—one that wouldn't involve killing my flowers; but I couldn't find anything. After all,

Dad is mostly blind. So I decided right then and there: Dad would water. He mattered the most. I wanted him to be happy. That's what I really wanted.

The carpets soon fell into his domain as well. As summer turned to fall and Dad moved from outside to inside, he took over the vacuuming chores. Nobody is more meticulous than he. He goes over each carpet segment from five different directions. A job that would normally take thirty minutes now takes three hours. First, he sucks up the dirt. Then, for the next two-and-a-half hours, he sucks up the color. I think he may be pulling electrons out of their orbit. One day our living room may go nuclear.

Of course, having the vacuum scream for hours on end isn't exactly pleasant. Nowadays, we schedule ourselves to be out of the house whenever Dad drags out the Hoover. Once again, we could have told him no, but when we asked what we really wanted, Dad won the vacuuming job.

My guess is that after viewing our home for the first time you wouldn't be able to explain why our plants look so bad while the carpets look so good. You'd have to know two important facts. First, when caught between competing priorities, I've learned to step back from the fray and ask what I really want. Second, I love my dad. The combined effect of these two seemingly unrelated facts is actually quite wonderful.

Dad is flourishing, and that's all I really want.

AUDIO DOWNLOAD: Listen to Kerry tell his story, "What Do You Really Want?"

To access an MP3 download of Kerry narrating this story, as well as other free resources from *The Gray Fedora*, visit **www.vitalsmarts.com/bookresources**.

LIFE'S A SPEECH

///

"If my films make one more person
miserable, I'll feel I have done my job."

WOODY ALLEN

W hen John Belushi and Dan Aykroyd started rehearsing the
1981 film *Neighbors*, one of the greatest casting errors in the
history of movies was set into motion. True to type, John had been
cast as the zany neighbor, Dan as the conservative one. For reasons
only the two of them will ever know, Belushi and Aykroyd insisted
on reversing roles. Now, thousands of fans would be able to watch
John Belushi—the greatest maniac of all time—acting controlled
and normal. What a disaster. By the time the director shouted,
"It's a wrap," everyone associated with the film was convinced they
had just created a train wreck that couldn't be saved in post.

Sure enough, when the producers previewed the movie with
audiences, they quickly learned that John Q. Public wasn't in love
with the new movie, hated the fact that John Belushi was the normal character, and were generally underwhelmed. Critics universally panned the film.

To avoid losing their investment, producers came up with a
scheme that served as a marketing model for years to come. They
chose to hype the movie with a deluge of ads for the two weeks
immediately preceding the first showing—spending the entire
marketing budget early on, because there would be no later on.
The plan worked. Hordes of adoring fans went to see Aykroyd

and Belushi opening night, and for the first couple of weeks the producers earned their money back. And then the movie tanked as people told their friends not to go.

As this was going on in Hollywood, 1,370 miles away in Detroit, I was about to give a speech. Fortunately, the audience I'd be facing was made up of people who didn't expect much from me as a speaker. I met their expectations—delivering a presentation that was lukewarm at best.

Then, to my surprise, I was invited to give the speech again—apparently, I was the only game in town. Based on the reaction to the first speech, I now had an inkling of what the audience liked and disliked. So I altered a few slides, added a story here, clipped a silence-inducing concept there, and eventually delivered a greatly improved presentation.

Based on this upgraded performance, my speaking requests skyrocketed. Soon I was giving weekly presentations all around the country—each speech benefiting from the previous. By the time *Neighbors* was pulled from the theaters and critics had hurled their last invective, I was being heralded as a decent orator who delivered a crackerjack speech.

As I've thought about these two events, my heart goes out to filmmakers. Producers spend tens of millions on a production, show it to audiences, and then wait for the fallout. There's not much they can do if it doesn't go well. The sets have been demolished, the people behind the cameras have moved on to new projects, and the principal actors have scattered to the wind. With a movie, you have one chance to get it right, and then it's on to the next one. At best, you can tweak a little here and cut a little there, but nothing more than that.

My speech, in contrast, provided ample opportunity for me to improve on my original disaster by running short-term mini-experiments. With each new speech, I'd try out new ideas or methods, watch the reaction, make changes, test them, and then repeat the process until—by golly—I had a finely tuned, widely accepted finished product. In fact, that's not even true. With a speech, you *never* have a finished product. With each new delivery, you're provided one more opportunity to make improvements based on your latest audience's reaction.

And now, the reason this is all relevant. From 1980 until now, I have received hundreds of papers from students and dozens of projects from young people I work with developing training products. I have observed that far too often, individuals approach creative tasks as if they were producing a movie. They work hard to create a finished product and hand it to me—ta-da!—never (or only barely) having tested it with an audience and too late to be altered.

I suppose we develop this "life is a movie" attitude early on in our education. We work on our first science project or term paper, hand it in, and pray for a good grade. We're lucky to get it handed in at all, let alone tested, changed, polished, and refined. As a result, by the time I work with students in graduate school, they're used to dashing out a project, doing the least amount possible to receive the grade they want, and then moving on. They have neither the time nor the inclination to polish anything.

Unfortunately, when it comes to producing a noteworthy product, polishing is everything. Just ask professional writers about their craft. They'll eagerly tell you, "Writing is rewriting." And if they're smart, they're rewriting based on the reaction of members of their target audience. This lesson can be hard learned. I have a talented friend whose published book was universally criticized for being slow-moving and lengthy. When I asked what had happened, he sheepishly reported that only his editors had read the book before it was released—and then solely for grammar.

Life is a speech, not a movie. We're almost always given a chance to rework our projects. Unlike movie makers, people who collaborate with us don't disappear into the wind. It doesn't cost millions to return to our initial work. It just takes the guts and humility to share our ideas with others—early on—and then ask for honest feedback.

For instance, when we develop a new training product, we don't create two days of training and then test it with a beta group. We work feverishly on one hour of the training and then test it. Then we make changes and test it again and again. Next we combine two one-hour segments into a quarter day. By the time we release a finished product, every element has been vetted by real audiences, dozens of times.

Working and reworking a project until it appears professional, smooth, and "effortless" can be misleading to the casual observer. When I first saw Woody Allen perform a stand-up routine on *The Tonight Show*, I was astonished by his ability to deliver one hilarious joke after another. Years later, I learned that before performing that remarkable set, he had put together ten jokes and tried them out at a local club. One joke survived. Then he tried out ten more and then another ten, until he had the "effortless" set he delivered on TV. Mr. Allen understood that he wasn't producing a movie, he was giving a speech, and a speech can be easily tested and improved until the finished product looks effortless.

Understanding this idea gives us hope. It helps free us from the frightening challenge of "getting it right the first time." Instead, when it comes to working on complex projects, we should produce a first draft, run tests, make changes, and repeat. So I'll say it one more time: Life is a speech, not a movie.

And thank goodness for that.

WHAT HAPPENED TO LUCY?

////////////////////////////

"If a man does not keep pace with his
companions, perhaps it is because he
hears a different drummer."

HENRY DAVID THOREAU

W hen I received notification from a committee of former high
school friends that my class would be holding its forty-year
reunion, I could hardly wait. My family moved away from town
the year I graduated, and I hadn't seen anybody since. I was desperate to return home and thank all the people who had been such
good friends growing up.

I wanted to thank Rob Bostick for driving me around when
he could drive and I couldn't. So I did. I wanted to thank Buck
O'Shannon for sticking up for me one day in the seventh grade
when a ninth-grade bully was pushing me around and Buck (who
was shaving by age eleven) "intervened" on my behalf. I thanked
him profusely.

For three hours I pushed my way through the crowd—recon-
necting, reliving, and thanking. But something was missing. As the
night progressed, I couldn't find the classmate I was certain would
have lived the most interesting life after high school. I'll call her
Lucy. I fell under her spell in the seventh grade after several grade
schools had merged their graduates into one seventh-grade class.

Lucy had come from an expensive private school where the kids were more socially mature and intellectually advanced than the ignorant alumni of my elementary school. Lucy and her former classmates were into algebra and Latin. My classmates and I were fascinated by small, shiny objects.

As luck would have it, Lucy sat behind me in our seventh-grade homeroom class and immediately stole my heart. Sadly, I had no hope of winning her affection, because I was from the wrong side of the tracks. My dad worked for a few dimes over minimum wage; her dad was a prominent lawyer. Our house had one bedroom and sat next to a swamp. Her three-story mansion had a tennis court that sat next to an atrium. I had never heard the word *atrium*.

Every school day, I turned from my desk in front of Lucy and stared into her beautiful brown eyes—not enough to alert the authorities; just enough to be creepy. Luckily, Lucy was too refined to be rude to me. She never complained.

Lucy was also a brilliant student. For six years, she meticulously prepared herself to head to one of the big-name colleges in the Northeast that I had only heard about in movies. I played around until the week before college commenced, when I hastily applied to a junior college in Idaho. Lucy went to one of the "Seven Sisters." I studied potatoes.

Lucy was also a model citizen. You could routinely find her in the hallways helping new students find their way or raising funds for the homeless. I spent most of my free time leaning up against the main hallway wall, where I bit off the ends of a black licorice twist (turning it into a pea shooter) and then bit off additional pieces of licorice and shot them onto the sweater of any girl who walked within range.

In short, Lucy was rich, smart, and kind. I was poor, dim-witted, and . . . well, a teenage boy. And yet, despite being separated by a hopelessly wide social chasm, Lucy was always kind to me. In return, I gave her the best I had to offer. I never fired a chunk of licorice at her.

And now for the peculiar part of this story. Nobody at my reunion could tell me where Lucy was or what had happened to her. Obviously, I wouldn't know what had happened; I had resided hundreds of miles away for forty years. But the people who had never left town didn't know anything about Lucy, either. How could the most accomplished and conspicuous person in our class, from the most prominent family in town, have vanished?

As the reunion was drawing to a close, a classmate finally offered up some news about Lucy. He had run into her in the local bookstore some thirty years earlier. She had been dressed in tattered hippy clothes (this would have been a full decade after the movement) while carrying a baby in a sling. And then he kicked me in the gut with the news that Lucy and child had *hitchhiked* across the country. I had to sit down as I lamented over the image of her, babe in arms, thumbing a ride across the country. What had happened?

I realize it's easy to come back with, "Hey, just because Lucy didn't end up the president or a corporate lawyer is no reason to be alarmed." But a twenty-eight-year-old woman had hitchhiked three thousand miles with a baby. How could this story ever be given a feel-good spin?

It only grew worse. I learned from the very last person I talked to at the reunion that Lucy was now living across the country in a one room shack with no electricity. Lucy. Sweet, kind, hope-of-America Lucy.

My mind swirled as I tried to process the image of the finest girl I had known staring into a kerosene lantern. At first I cursed the horrendous toll that had been paid by my generation—the first to be invited straight out of high school into a countrywide drug movement. Worse still, Lucy had moved to a school that made fun of everything her parents had held dear.

I pictured professors admonishing Lucy to reject "The Man," new friends ridiculing her small-town ways, classmates dropping a hallucinogenic substance into her drink. Surely one or all of these things had combined forces to drive Lucy down a path that took her to a point where she eventually begged her way across America with a baby.

Next I wanted to help. I know—maybe Lucy was fine. But all I could see in my mind's eye was an image of her sitting alone in a shack—and I wasn't picturing Thoreau; I was picturing a hobo. But what could I do? What should I do? I wanted to board a plane or write a check or punch somebody. I wanted to do *something*.

Eventually an idea came to me. Why not return to my original plan? I vowed to thank the people who had been such good friends. I hadn't run into Lucy, so I would write her a letter. Nothing fancy. No need to talk about her last forty years or mine. Just a brief explanation of how I had promised to thank people who had been kind to me—and that certainly included her.

Usually when I'm feeling blue I work hard to make things better. Not this time. I didn't try to fix anything. Instead, in a heartfelt letter, I thanked Lucy for not treating me as a kid from the wrong side of the tracks, despite the fact that I was, in every sense of the words, from the wrong side of the tracks.

Thank you, Lucy. Thanks for giving a pesky kid a chance. May your kind acts toward me and others have filled your life with happiness.

Update. After decades of no hometown contact, Lucy recently attended a reunion held by her elementary school. One of her classmates informed me that after years of wandering, Lucy had finally settled in as the owner/manager of a hospice. She and other like-minded staff members provide love and care for terminal patients. If you've ever placed a family member in a hospice, you know that it's the job for an angel. It's a job for Lucy. Sweet, hope-of-America Lucy.

THE MERCHANT OF BELLINGHAM

///

"You don't have to have a college degree to
serve. . . you only need a heart full of grace."

MARTIN LUTHER KING, JR.

During WWII, my father worked for Boeing as the team leader
of a group of craftsmen. He and his team produced the mech-
anism that makes it possible to lower bomber landing gear by
hand—needed only should something go wrong with the auto-
mated equipment. If you've seen old movies of frantic airmen trying to lower their landing gear by hand before touching down on
an open field, then you know the contribution my dad and his
team made to the war effort.

When the war came to an end and there was no longer a need
for life-saving bomber equipment, Dad was out of a job. One day
he came up with the idea of owning and operating a small grocery
store—the kind of mom-and-pop operation you could find about
every six blocks in the mid-40s.

As it turned out, Dad wasn't cut out for such employment. So
Grandpa took charge. He moved in, we moved out, and over the
next twenty years, my grandfather, a fiery, five-foot-two Irishman
with a cigar stub perennially stuck in the corner of his mouth,

became "Pop" to everyone who stopped by the store to pick up a loaf of bread and chat about the weather.

One day, when I asked Grandpa what he called himself (I knew what he did, I just didn't know what to call it), he told me he was a "merchant." I haven't heard anyone use that term since then, but when Grandpa claimed the title, it was clear that a merchant was something special. He always dressed in wool suit pants, a white shirt and tie, and a pale green apron. Whether he was candling eggs, putting away redeemable bottles, or standing patiently as a child picked out five cents' worth of penny candy, Grandpa attacked the task with the pride and precision of a physician performing surgery. After all, he was a merchant.

I remember watching Grandpa patiently wait on people of every ilk—even though many of his patrons were of questionable "ilkage." Since Grandpa's store was located in a financially challenged neighborhood, there was no telling who would walk in the door or what that person might require.

Among the motley collection of customers who frequented "Pop's" store, several individuals with learning challenges found their way to his establishment almost every day. The ritual was always the same. Lacking the skills and confidence that comes from being literate, they'd shyly point at the items they wanted, reach into their pocket, and pull out a handful of crumpled bills and loose coins. Then, without making a big deal of it, Grandpa would pick out the correct amount of money, bag the groceries, and send the customer on his or her way with a heartfelt, "Thank you."

Grandpa had spent the first forty years of his career as a bit of a celebrity in the lumber business. He was such a whiz with numbers that he could walk through an entire lumber mill and keep track of the board footage in his head. He had earned a great deal of respect performing these calculations, so you might suspect that in his senior years he'd find the task of waiting on people to be beneath him. But he didn't. Grandpa often told me it was an honor, even noble, to help others meet their needs. After all, he was a merchant.

People counted on Grandpa, and Grandpa knew it. After my first year of college, I prepared to travel abroad for two years. One day, and at the very last minute, I asked Grandpa to attend my going-away speech at church. Now, Grandpa kept his store open thirteen hours a day, seven days a week, so you can imagine his reply. His countenance shifted into utter shock, "I can't close the store! What if Mrs. Eherenfieldt needs some cheese for her casserole? Or what if Ronnie Keebler falls and skins his knee? Where will Mrs. Keebler get a Band-Aid?"

My father had made precision landing gear that saved entire bomber crews. Grandpa provided cheddar cheese and Band-Aids. But he saw himself as equally important. And you know what? He was.

Along with the cheese and Band-Aids, Grandpa doled out friendly banter and helpful advice. I remember watching him celebrate with a young man who had just been admitted to a prestigious college. Grandpa had watched him grow up. He was a penny-candy kid who had excelled in math, and Grandpa saw him as one of his protégés. Grandpa had taught him math tricks. It was all part of the services rendered at Noonan's Grocery.

Sometimes people came to the store, glanced around nervously, and then timidly whispered in Grandpa's ear. Years later, I learned that they had been asking for credit. They needed food for their tables, didn't have cash, and Grandpa would be the one to lend a hand.

Over the years, I overheard adults criticizing Grandpa for extending credit to people to whom nobody else would ever float a loan. Most of his patrons paid him back. However, there were enough who didn't that Grandpa didn't make much of a profit. When I asked him about the practice of extending bad loans, he smiled knowingly and explained that his mission covered more than simply making money.

As I stopped by the store one day to pick up a loaf of bread, two rather somber-looking gentlemen in dark suits were exiting.

"Those fellows were FBI agents," Grandpa explained. "They come by every once in a while when one of the locals applies for a federal job that calls for a background investigation. They talk to me about the candidate. You know, did he steal stuff as a kid? Things like that."

Grandpa loved being a merchant who sat in the social and commercial center of the neighborhood—partly because of the nature of the job and partly because he simply loved to work. Long before people would write books about customer service, Grandpa delivered it seven days a week for more than twenty years. It came not from techniques, tricks, or algorithms, but from a genuine respect for all those he served. He thought service was noble—never confusing providing service with being servile.

Grandpa kept up his earnest efforts until, at age eighty-eight, he suffered a stroke and fell to the floor. He had been fetching a bottle of soda pop for Tim Harmon, a young man who had grown up hanging out at the store. Tim ran out the front door and flagged down a passing car. Then he gently cradled Grandpa in his arms until an ambulance arrived. "Pop" had fallen. Tim, loving him like a member of his own family, gently comforted the man who had served so many for so long.

"Call the bread man and ask him to remove the stock from the shelves. It'll go bad," Grandpa managed to utter as the ambulance pulled off. "We can't be selling stale bread. Mrs. Eherenfieldt will never be satisfied with stale bread."

Such were the last words of the Merchant of Bellingham.

//////////////////////// **3** ////////////////////////

BUSINESS LESSONS

THE LAW OF THE HOG

//

". . . if you wrong us, shall we not revenge?"

WILLIAM SHAKESPEARE

W hen David Maxfield and I pulled up to the plywood mill, we were surprised to see an ambulance parked out front. We had come to study the impact of an upcoming leadership-training program, but I must admit it was difficult to think about research as we walked by a vehicle that had "Sisters of Mercy Hospital" painted on both sides in large, red letters.

Our guess was that an employee had suffered an accident. After all, the place sported gigantic saw blades, menacing debarkers, and a terrifying machine known as "the hog." Which, by the way, you're not allowed to go near, unless you wear a safety belt that keeps you from falling into a hole in the floor that leads to an assortment of razor-sharp, spinning blades.

As it turns out, there had been no accident. According to the HR manager who was now taking us on a tour of the facility, Tony, a supervisor on the graveyard shift, had confronted Max, an hourly employee who wasn't following correct procedures. Max disagreed. One thing led to another until Max pushed Tony, who pushed back, and then Max fell and cut a large gash in his forehead.

"But we're trying to turn that around," explained the HR manager. "That's why we're implementing a leadership training program. We want you to help us determine if the instruction we'll be providing actually works."

As Max was loaded into the ambulance, David and I walked to the main conference room just down the hall. There, scattered around a table, sat eight randomly selected employees who had been scheduled to talk with us about what it was like working in a plywood mill. This was to be the first of two dozen such group interviews.

As I cleared my throat to start the conversation, on cue, the ambulance driver sounded the siren. Everyone turned to the window to watch the emergency vehicle haul their coworker away. Then, in unison, the eight employees turned their heads back toward David and me and shot us a look that said, "What do you think of the place so far?"

By now I was aching to know what these employees thought about the shoving match that had just occurred. So I asked, "What happens around this place if you dislike how you've been treated by one of your leaders?" After a brief pause, a fellow looked me in the eye, smiled contemptuously, and uttered two words that to this day reverberate in my mind: "The hog!"

As the blood drained from my face, I managed to ask, "You mean that machine with the nasty blades you use to cut up scrap veneer?"

"Exactly!" he replied.

By now, I was envisioning a team of angry employees wrestling their foreman to the ground and stuffing him into that frightening hole in the floor. "So, precisely what do you mean when you say 'the hog'?" I continued as I prayed for an answer that didn't involve death and dismemberment.

"When our boss leaves our work area, we take perfectly good veneer and throw it into the hog," one of the interviewees answered politely.

"That's right," another employee chimed in. "The hog is used for chopping up scrap. When someone grinds up good veneer, it hurts the foreman's numbers. That gets the foreman in trouble with the plant manager."

"Absolutely. If you want to get even with a supervisor who's just insulted you or tried to jerk you around," explained still another interviewee, "you feed the hog."

It was from this incident that David and I created the expression "The Law of the Hog." It means that if you talk with someone who has disappointed you or behaved poorly, but you do so in a way that is less than professional, others may find a way to get even—i.e., "feed the hog."

Over the years, we've learned that every organization has its own version of feeding the hog. In one freight-shipping company, employees upset at being mistreated threw perfectly good parts into the deep blue sea. At a computer chip manufacturer, disgruntled associates flushed gold chips down the toilet. At a software company, angry code writers purposely wrote errors into the program. These acts of sabotage were a means of seeking revenge on the leaders.

Of course, not everyone who believes he or she has been treated poorly seeks such direct and active revenge. The most common method of feeding the hog takes the form of lost focus, energy, and engagement. After being harshly treated by a leader, employees spend time talking about what just happened rather than doing their job. Next, they refuse to put in extra effort. Eventually, they disengage.

But there's more to the hog story. Years later, I asked David (who had talked extensively with Tony, the abusive supervisor) how Tony felt about the incident.

"Don't you know?" replied David. "He was devastated. He had worked at the mill for years. When he was finally promoted to foreman, he discovered that it was difficult to get people to listen to him. He desperately wanted employees to follow procedures and meet deadlines, but they often ignored him.

"With time," David continued, "he learned to rely on intimidation, but he hated doing so. It was a small town. Some of Tony's direct reports were neighbors, others relatives, and now they all saw him as the enemy. Tony's own wife refused to go to church with him or otherwise be seen with him in public."

So this wasn't merely a story of aggression followed by revenge. Tony wasn't the bad guy, and the employees weren't innocent bystanders exacting justice. It was a more complex tale about creating a culture of accountability.

Fortunately, the leadership training we were hired to study actually did teach foremen how to hold others accountable. By learning best practices, Tony and the other leaders discovered what many skilled leaders had known for years. When you carefully study how to hold others accountable, and then actually use the skills you've learned, you don't have to rely on intimidation, threats, and abuse. You can deal with deviations and disappointments without feeding the hog.

And, unless you're the hog, that's a good thing.

~

VIDEO: The Law of the Hog

To access a live-action portrayal of "The Law of the Hog", as well as other free resources from *The Gray Fedora*, visit **www.vitalsmarts.com/bookresources**.

FEELING FRAZZLED?

///

"There's no such thing as work-life balance. There
are work-life choices, and you make them,
and they have consequences."

JACK WELCH

In early 1951, a few months before I entered the first grade, the
U. S. embarked on one of the most peculiar and troubling lines of
research ever conducted. Sixty-five miles northwest of Las Vegas,
in a place known as the Nevada Proving Grounds, scientists began
detonating nuclear devices. You know, to see what would happen.

I first became aware of these frightening blasts when Mrs.
Kavonavitch, our grade-school principal, started projecting movie
clips from the Nevada test site onto the cafeteria wall. After each
nuclear display ended, Mrs. Kavonavitch blew a whistle, and
we feverishly scattered about the room like—well, like kids in a
nuclear-attack drill.

After careening about wildly, trying our best not to lose a shoe,
we eventually found an empty spot on the edge of the floor. There
we lay facedown, placed our hands tightly behind our necks, and
imagined our faces melting from the searing heat of the unholy
mushroom cloud that would soon roll over our beloved cafeteria.

One day, the newsreel flickering on the wall showed something
new. It was American soldiers dressed in fatigues, toting rifles and
holding their helmets tightly to their heads as they walked into a

cloud of nuclear dust—to measure the impact of, well, marching directly into a cloud of nuclear dust.

If you were to view this same footage today, you'd surely ask, "What are those scientists doing to those poor soldiers?" It's not as if the dangers of radiation were a secret. Certainly not in 1951. Yet the testing continued.

If you're the least bit cautious, you can't watch this "science-gone-mad" video without asking, "What similarly insane things are we doing today?" What modern inventions have we wholly embraced, that appear to have made our lives better, but are actually slowly killing us? In short, what "nuclear walk" are we taking today?

I have a candidate for a technological trend I suspect fits the bill. Should you take a vacation nowadays with a couple dozen adults of differing ages and backgrounds, you would note that they fall into two groups. First, those who set aside their worries, take their minds off their jobs, and throw themselves into the true spirit of vacationing. That's Group One, and it's small.

The people in the larger Group Two offer up the occasional "Ooh!" or "Ahh!" but they aren't exactly living in the moment—primarily because they haven't actually unplugged from their jobs. They're digitally linked to their offices—constantly fidgeting with their electronic devices, dashing off texts, and whispering underneath the tour guide's lecture.

It wasn't always this way. As I prepared to depart on my first overseas vacation thirty years ago, my boss kindly exhorted, "Please don't phone us. Don't even think about us. If you call us, it'll take you a full day to get back into vacation mode. Disconnect, relax, and recharge your batteries. We'll take care of whatever comes up."

Contrast this thoughtful advice with the experience of two of my friends, Sofia and Makai. Their bosses—like many of today's leaders—don't offer a comforting speech as their employees head out for a week of family fun. Their bosses insist that they respond to phone calls, e-mails, and texts twenty-four-seven—*especially* during vacations.

Of course, much of this torture is self-imposed. There are advantages to being able to connect to work, no matter your location. For one, you gain flexibility. You can take a mid-afternoon break to attend a niece's soccer game and then make up for lost time by connecting to your office and working from home later that evening. Plus, if you stay tethered, you can promptly respond to phone calls, e-mails, tweets, and texts. Everyone appreciates that.

But what if you unplugged from the grid once in a while? Would disconnecting for an hour or so actually make your life better? In a word, yes. Consider the effects of constant interruptions. Every time you stop your current task, deal with an interruption, and then return, you place the original task from short- to long-term memory, put the new job into short-term memory, and then reverse the entire process to get back on task. Completing this conceptual juggling act dozens of times a day creates stress, which just might lead to distress and all of its attendant health problems.

Frequent interruptions can also lead to job dissatisfaction. Instead of working continuously for periods of an hour or more on a task that's challenging and solvable (elements that career expert Mihály Csikszentmihályi insists contribute to job satisfaction), we purposely interrupt our flow, add stress, and make our jobs less satisfying.

On those occasions when blurring the borders between work and home leads to additional time on the job, this too can exact a hefty toll. In a study conducted in England, those who labored eleven or more hours per day had a 67 percent higher risk of coronary heart disease than their less-tethered nine-to-five office mates.

Even if you don't work extended hours, the mere act of remaining connected can be surprisingly damaging. Waiting to be interrupted—*expecting* to be interrupted—can trigger a stress response similar to that of actually being disturbed, even when no interruption occurs.

Obviously, with the release of each new innovation, there's much to consider. As we invent and embrace new devices, we may not know the toll they're taking on our mental, emotional, and physical health until it's too late. Whether we're setting ourselves up for job dissatisfaction, family tension, or failing health is difficult to anticipate.

To help turn this around, make the current practice of remaining constantly tethered and frequently interrupted part of your family and corporate dialogue. Talk openly about the two-edged sword of innovation. What new invention or trend is working for you? What's slowly killing you? Decide how and when you want to be connected and where and when you want to be interrupted. Make it a choice, not an automatic assumption you make when embracing a tool that is helpful in some areas but may be deadly in others.

The good news is that it's not an all-or-nothing proposition. No one is required to take a vow of digital celibacy. You don't have to become a Luddite and surrender your devices; you simply have to control them, so they don't control you. For instance, you can set your devices to notify you only at certain times, as opposed to the instant a message arrives. You can also negotiate with colleagues and bosses to watch your back while you vacation, disconnect, and recharge your batteries.

Friends can and should be part of the solution rather than part of the problem. Friends don't let friends blindly walk into a nuclear cloud.

AND ONE FOR TANYA

"Finding good players is easy. Getting them
to play as a team is another story."

CASEY STENGEL

On December 25th of 2007, my daughter Rebecca hugged her
two-year-old son, Timmy; kissed her husband, Bruce; boarded
a jumbo jet; and started a journey that would forever alter their
lives. A few months earlier, she and her husband had become
aware of two orphan girls in Russia—Nika, aged seven, and Tanya,
aged five—who were scheduled to be sent to different orphanages
and very likely would be lost to each other forever if they were not
adopted soon.

Rebecca and Bruce decided that they would start the adoption
process. Of course, before they could do anything, someone would
have to meet the two girls and see if the adoption was both possible and the right thing to do—thus Rebecca's arduous Christ-
mas-day flight.

Nika and Tanya practically jumped out of their skin when they
first met Rebecca—such was their excitement after living in an
orphanage for more than a year without so much as a single visitor
or prospective parent ever stopping to see them. Nika had learned
three English words, "I love you," while Tanya, the shyer of the
two, communicated by staring at Rebecca through large, twinkly
brown eyes. Both showed off their ability to perform somersaults,
sing Russian folk songs, and daringly leap off chairs as they des-

perately auditioned for the role of daughter. At one point, Nika suggested through her interpreter, "If you become our mommy, we'll wash the dishes every day."

With these sweet words, Rebecca's heart nearly broke. Right then and there, she started the mountain of paperwork that would eventually culminate in two frightened little Russian girls flying to America to start a new life—forever grafted onto the Patterson and Westenskow family trees.

I met Nika and Tanya four months later, when the two rail-thin waifs finally arrived in America. They had been playing with their new cousins in our backyard when Nika rushed up to me and gestured that she was thirsty. I had purchased cans of apple juice for just such an occasion and offered her one.

Nika punched in the flip-top and in lizard-like fashion, darted her tongue into the opening to test the liquid. Approving of the juice with a quick smile, she then gestured for a second can for her little sister. Tanya was playing nearby with a doll and didn't appear thirsty, but Nika asked anyway.

Several years have passed since that day, and the ritual hasn't changed much. Nika can speak fluent English now, but with each item of food or drink someone offers her, she holds out her hand and firmly requests, "And one for Tanya." I'm pretty sure that after the expression "I love you," these were the first English words Nika learned.

When Rebecca initially spoke with the girls' caseworker, she learned that their mother had raised them for a time but had then turned them over to her parents. Two years after that, the aging grandparents sent them to an orphanage. That was about all we knew of their childhood, until one day when Rebecca was showing Nika how their new blender worked and casually asked if her grandparents had owned a similar appliance. Nika stared at her mother, blinked slowly as she thought about what to say, and then answered, "No, we didn't have a blender. We had only one electric light. We didn't always have running water, and the toilet was outside."

Then Nika offered the following heartbreaking addendum: "We were hungry all the time. I went door-to-door and begged from the neighbors. Sometimes they would give me a bit of cabbage or a piece of carrot, and I would run home and share it with Tanya."

Eventually, the neighbors could stand it no longer. Watching the two little girls slowly starve was more than they could bear, so they turned the children in to the authorities, who immediately placed them in a hospital. While there, nutritionists stuffed them full of calories for two weeks before they were finally placed in an orphanage.

So there it was. At age five, Nika had become the caregiving adult in her tragic little community. Even now, when surrounded by a greater number of caring adults than she had probably ever imagined, she still watched out for her younger sister. Just in case. Whenever she's given anything, she sets her jaw and firmly requests, "And one for Tanya."

I've learned a great deal from Nika and other such selfless souls. They not only make good siblings and friends, they make wonderful teammates. In fact, they're the kind of people employees look for when forming a team. Ask employees what they look for in a teammate, and they invariably respond, "Someone to watch my back." The same holds for friends.

Healthy families and personal relationships are built of such stuff—people caring for each other, thinking of others, watching out for loved ones and coworkers, and even taking the occasional lump for one another.

I've experienced this type of selfless treatment firsthand. I once designed and tested a training course in which each new group I instructed would grudgingly file into a training room, sit stoically in their seats, and scowl. Peering out into the audience was like staring at an angry oil painting.

A federal judge had mandated the training, and now I was delivering it to an unwilling audience while internal training specialists sat in the back row and ridiculed everything I did. All of this took place while I fought a flu virus that had so weakened my system, I frequently had to lean against the wall for support in order to continue with the training.

As I lay on the floor in my motel room at the end of that first day, working to produce the next day's version of the training, I heard a knock. I made my way to the door, opened it, and in burst David, my business partner.

David had heard of my plight, and instead of calling to ask if I needed help, he had boarded a plane. He sent me home to get better and then prepared to stand before the angry audiences and take my licking. For the next three days, he took on the angry oil painting. He never mentioned his sacrifice to me, let alone asked for anything in return.

What do these experiences teach us? What should one look for in a teammate, business partner, or maybe even a life partner? One thing's for certain: You should definitely seek someone like David—a person who stands beside you through thick and thin, jumps to your aid when needed, and takes a licking for you.

Now that I've met Nika, I have an additional recommendation. Find someone like her as well. *Be* someone like her. When others are carping about their workload or bickering over who gets the biggest piece of the pie, be the person who steps up and says, "And one for Tanya."

We'll all be forever blessed.

JUST WHAT THE MILKMAN ORDERED

///

"People don't listen when you lecture. No one
wants to be talked down to or scolded."

SCOTT THOMPSON

In the late spring of 1954, two important events overlapped—
Mother's Day and the arrival of the carnival. Since both required
considerable money, I had to save for months. By hoarding my
weekly allowance of fifty cents, I was able to set aside six whole
dollars—two dollars to buy my mom the Mother's Day earrings
she had pointed out to me in a jewelry store window, two dollars
for an unlimited carnival ride pass, and two dollars for food and
bus fare.

When I got off the bus the day the carnival arrived, I set off to
buy Mom's earrings before the rides gobbled me up. Regrettably,
as I walked toward the jeweler, the sound of children screaming
in delight was more than I could withstand. I abandoned my mission to buy my mother's earrings and instead bolted to the fanciful
home of the Tilt-A-Whirl. This was my first mistake.

I made my second mistake when I arrived at the carnival. Instead
of going directly to the ticket booth and buying my unlimited ride
pass, I wandered into the midway, where a horde of carnies vied
for my money. I resisted the temptation to toss balls, rings, and the

like until I came across a booth that awarded, of all things, parakeets as prizes.

I had never seen such exquisite birds before. They were bright blue and green—almost fluorescent—and better yet, you could teach them to talk. Imagine that, a talking bird! Surely Mom would like one of these feathered miracles far more than any stupid old earrings! Plus, all I had to do to win was toss a dime and land it on a plate. And the plates were huge!

So I eagerly cashed in a dollar for ten dimes. The first one hit right on a plate—oh boy, oh boy, oh boy! But then it bounced off. No big deal. It *almost* landed on another plate. This was going to be easy.

After bouncing another six dimes and always coming close but never winning anything, I started to walk away until the helpful fellow who worked the booth told me not to worry; I was bound to win soon. Now, this advice was coming from an official carnival employee who carried a pack of Lucky Strikes neatly tucked under his right T-shirt sleeve. Surely a man of such impeccable fashion sense and elevated status in the community knew what he was talking about.

And so went the two dollars I had set aside for food and return bus fare. But hold on, I thought to myself, if I won a bird, I could replace it with the money I'd set aside for the earrings and I'd be back on budget. The next twenty dimes bounced pretty much like the first twenty.

As I tightened my hold on my last two dollars, I headed toward the jewelry store before it was too late. But I didn't make it. Just as I turned to leave, one of the parakeets chirped, "Pretty bird!" (at least I thought it did), and that's all it took. With one good toss I'd win the best dang Mother's Day present ever! It would be epic.

The three-mile walk home that day was a miserable one. I hadn't eaten anything, I hadn't gotten to go on a single ride, I didn't have a Mother's Day present, and I was going to get into serious trouble when my parents found out that I had literally thrown away my money.

As I walked down the last half mile of the dirt road that led home, my next-door neighbor, Oscar Jensen, drove up in his milk truck. Oscar arose every day at the crack of dawn and delivered milk to mom-and-pop stores and families around town. He was now on his way home. Normally, I would have been thrilled to hitch a ride. You know, ride up front with a guy wearing a milkman uniform and white hat; maybe even eat a free Fudgsicle. But not this day. I wanted no such nonsense. After all, I had just suffered the great parakeet fiasco of 1954.

One look at my countenance and Mr. Jensen could tell I was distraught. As I told him about the stunning birds I wanted to win, I confided that I'd lost all my money. He nodded knowingly but didn't say a word. Eventually, when we pulled up to his house, he turned to me and said, "I've done you a good turn by giving you a ride home; would you do something for me? I've just had a new load of furnace wood delivered, and I need some of it chopped into kindling." Then he handed me a large, sharp ax.

Now, before you go all safety-conscious on me, allow me to remind you that this took place in 1954. Back then, eight-year-old boys went to the carnival unaccompanied, walked long distances alone, and, yes, even swung the occasional ax. I did, anyway.

After a couple of hours, Oscar reappeared, gave my stack of kindling a nod of approval, and said it was getting late and I needed to go home. As I turned down the path that led to our house, I felt a tap on my shoulder. I looked around, and there stood Mr. Jensen holding out six one-dollar bills. "This is for the work you did," he uttered without embellishment. Then he turned and walked away.

Six dollars! At age eight, and on that particular day, it was like being handed six million dollars. I could hardly wait to get home and tell Mom what had happened.

Now, let's take a look at what Oscar had done. He heard the tale of how foolish I had been. He realized that my intentions were pure, but I had made an innocent mistake. However, he also figured that I had learned from the experience. Instead of lecturing me, he didn't say a negative word. Instead of keeping me from trying again, he set me up for another go around. He gave me a do-over.

When I returned to town the next morning, six dollars in hand, I went straight to the jewelry store. I bought the two-dollar earrings Mom wanted, which she wore on special occasions for the next fifty years. When I made my way over to the carnival, I didn't let myself walk within fifty feet of the parakeets. I knew I'd be too weak to resist the temptation. Avoiding the alluring call of "Pretty bird!" I bought a hank of cotton candy and an unlimited ride pass and spun myself into oblivion.

I learned several lessons that day. But the one I find most interesting was the one I learned from Mr. Jensen about leadership. When people who work for you make a mistake, stop and ask yourself what they really need. Did they have good intentions? Did they not know any better? Most importantly, have they learned their lesson and what they now need more than anything is another chance?

The next time someone messes up at work—or perhaps when one of your kids lets you down—and your natural inclination is to spout forth a lecture, think about Oscar and ask yourself, "Does this person need a do-over?"

Sometimes it's just what the milkman ordered.

TO EACH HIS OWN

"I can imagine nothing more terrifying than an eternity filled with men who were all the same."

T. H. WHITE

When Old Man Hoffmann pulled up in front of my grandfather's grocery store, he always caused a stir. That's because he didn't arrive in a car—or on a tractor, for that matter. No, when Old Man Hoffmann wanted to go somewhere, he hitched two draft horses to a hay wagon and trotted down the street.

Now if this equestrian feat wasn't sensational enough, his next act was even more amazing. The stoic German would climb down from the wagon, walk through the front door, march straight to the counter, and slap down a dime. Without a word, Grandpa would fetch his immigrant friend an ice-cold, ten-ounce bottle of Coca-Cola from the cooler.

Hoffmann would grab the bottle in his massive hand, take it to the wall that sported the bottle opener, and pop off the cap. Then he'd whip the Coke bottle to his lips, tilt it and his head back, and down the burning liquid in four or five gulps without so much as a single pause, belch, tear, or gasp for air. Then, to the cheering of the awestruck crowd of boys who gathered to witness this event (and who often attempted to recreate it), Hoffmann would smack the empty bottle down on the counter, turn on the heel of his boot, and head back home.

Even after the crowd dispersed, the encounter for me was far from over. When the old German climbed on his wagon, I'd try to sneak onto the back, where I would hide in a pile of loose hay. If he didn't spot me, I'd get a free ride home on a horse-drawn wagon. And that was fun.

Hoffmann wasn't into fun. He didn't like kids climbing on his wagon, and he let them know by turning his bullwhip on anyone who had the nerve to invade his space. On this particular day, as Hoffmann pulled away from the store, I quickly jumped on the back of his wagon and slid under a pile of fresh-cut hay. Eventually, I ventured out far enough from underneath the hay to dangle my legs off the back and enjoy the slow clip-clop of horse hooves as we rambled down the gravel road that passed in front of my house.

I should have known better than to sit out in the open. It wasn't long until a stray dog charged up the road, barking frantically at the two horses. When Mr. Hoffmann turned to give the mongrel a taste of his whip, he saw me sitting on his wagon, unharmed and with a stupid grin on my face. Offended by my impertinence, Hoffmann quickly changed targets by re-cocking his arm to give me a sharp smack.

Then fate stepped in. Before Mr. Hoffmann could whip me, we both heard a strange noise originating from somewhere up the road. In unison, we turned our attention to the ruckus. It was Dorothy, a middle-aged woman who lived nearby. Dorothy was not just one of those people who marched to the beat of a different drummer; she marched to the beat of a wildly *insane* drummer.

Whenever Dorothy walked up the road, she tilted forward as if struggling against a hurricane-force wind and she peered ahead until she saw another human being coming her way. Then, no matter the distance, Dorothy started shouting a garbled monologue that only she could understand.

Realizing that the chatter was just Dorothy, Mr. Hoffmann once again raised his right arm to give me a thrashing, but fate gave me another break. This time it was the sound of "Buggy Baker" bouncing down the rutted road in her war-surplus jeep.

Ms. Baker had earned the name Buggy because she was a high school biology teacher who loved bugs. Plus, she acted sort of buggy. For one, she drove an open jeep—not common for a woman in her fifties during the 50s. Two, she was always accompanied in her jeep by Billy, who was not only her best friend but, as his name might suggest, a goat.

On this day, as Buggy and Billy bounced down the road in her jeep, the hapless animal could hardly stay in the open space behind the front seat. Ms. Baker was driving far too fast on a road that was more pothole than path.

As Mr. Hoffmann and I paused to watch, it became clear that Buggy intended to pass the hay wagon at a dangerous clip. Just as Buggy began to hurl past us, Dorothy—still yammering away—stepped into the path of the careening jeep, and Buggy was forced to slam on the brakes.

As Buggy stomped on the pedal, the convulsing jeep pitched poor Billy into the open space to the right of the driver, legs splayed forward in the distinctly human pose of someone riding shotgun. The curiously embarrassed look on the goat's face was too funny for words.

As I looked at Old Man Hoffmann, he looked at Dorothy, Dorothy looked at Buggy, and we all grinned widely. Then, in a moment of truce, Hoffmann set down his whip, leaned back his head, and let out a howl that was half laugh, half choke. Buggy tittered, Dorothy cackled, and I laughed until tears ran down my cheeks.

When we finally came to our senses, Buggy shooed Billy to the back, carefully edged her jeep past the wagon, and pulled away. Dorothy leaned into the imaginary wind and strode off at full yammer. And, true to form, Hoffmann grabbed his whip to take one more crack at me.

Taking my cue, I leapt from the German's wagon and trotted the rest of the way home. Ten minutes later, I burst in our front door and excitedly told my mother the story of the goat that had been flipped to a point where it looked as if it were riding shotgun. Mom laughed along with me and then exclaimed, "Isn't it wonderful?"

"Isn't what wonderful?" I asked.

"Living in this neighborhood!" Mother explained. "We have people from all walks of life, and that makes this a perfect place to live." In my moment of near crisis, Mom chose to focus on the joys of diversity. She loved people of all shapes, looks, beliefs, and sizes. Here were three offbeat individuals whom many wouldn't have exactly welcomed as neighbors, and all Mom could think of was how interesting they were.

"To each his own." That had been Mom's mantra. Long before the virtues of diversity were being extoled in HR departments worldwide, Mom knew the joy that came from meeting, associating with, and loving people of every ethnicity, lifestyle, and belief.

Mom never changed. Decades later, on the eve of her death, I sat next to her as she knitted wool hats for the children of war-torn Bosnia—the *Encyclopedia Britannica* lying open next to her. "Bosnians!" Mom exclaimed. "Aren't they a fascinating bunch?"

Mom made diversity a wonderful thing.

BORDER GUARDS

///

"It is in the shelter of each other that the people live."

IRISH PROVERB

Unintended consequences—we've all experienced them. You have a well-intended idea, give it a whirl, and then something unpleasant results. For instance, you're trying to assist a colleague at work, and you inadvertently spill coffee on her desk. Or perhaps you help a friend rewrite a line of code and insert an error into the program. Or how about this? You point out that a new employee is doing something wrong, and he ends up getting dragged feet-first down a half dozen stairs while his head bangs on the cement steps. You know, stuff like that.

Now, about that stair incident. It was 1971. I had just been put in charge of the clothing locker located at the Coast Guard's boot camp in Alameda, California, and I had no idea what I was doing. It was our team's job to outfit new recruits with their uniforms. This would have been fairly easy, even for a newbie such as myself, had it not been for one tiny problem. We weren't the first to see the recruits. By the time we began our work with them, they were frightened to death. They would stand stiff and zombie-like and end up getting fitted poorly. A few weeks later they'd have to return to be refitted, and this was time-consuming and expensive. All of this could be resolved if we could encourage recruits to relax—be less zombie and more Gumby.

So I suggested to my boss that we stop the traditional practice of forcing initiates to strip down and stand naked at the beginning of the fitting. Standing naked in a large, cold room in front of dozens of other men seemed unsettling to me, and I wasn't even one of the naked ones. You would have thought I had suggested that we have the recruits put on prom dresses and dance with pigs.

"Not stand naked?" my boss exclaimed. "Why, it's tradition! If you want to build men, first you have to tear them down. What better way than through humiliation?"

"But we can't measure and fit them readily when they're humiliated and nervous," I explained. "What if we find a way to make the recruits laugh? You know, tell a joke or something. That might help the young men feel more at ease." So it was decided that I would "do something" to make the recruits laugh.

To get a feel for the humor quotient of the recruit audience we faced every week, consider what they did the five days *before* they marched into the clothing locker. From sunup to midnight, boot-pushers screamed at them nose to nose while calling them unflattering names such as maggot and puke, and not in the fun way you might find at a fraternity hazing—more like the evil way of a prison camp. Sometimes they were even marched into the estuary, rifles held over their heads, until someone nearly drowned.

As the next group of recruits dragged their terrified selves into the clothing locker, I was all set to tell a joke to get them to laugh, relax, and be easily measured. Luckily, an opportunity presented itself within minutes. As the platoon of sixty young men stood there sans clothing, I noticed that one of them was starting to put on his newly issued undershorts backward. Seizing the moment, I pointed out that the fellow in question didn't even know how to put on skivvies! Ha, ha, wasn't that a real stitch!

Granted, this wasn't exactly high comedy, but it was a start. Sadly, nobody laughed. Instead, fifty-nine pairs of eyes darted to the singled-out trainee—as if staring at a prisoner climbing the gallows. The boot-pusher who had been training this fine group of America's next lifesavers ran over to the skivvy-confused recruit and pushed the guy so hard that he fell backwards and knocked his head on the floor. The newbie was out like a light. Soon a medical team arrived, but after seeing that the injured party was "only a recruit," they grabbed the unconscious fellow by his feet, dragged him across the room and down the cement stairs—head bouncing all the way.

Good intentions—bad outcome. I had wanted people to relax but ended up putting a fellow in the infirmary. Fortunately, the young man quickly recovered and graduated with his unit, but no thanks to my half-baked plan. Additionally, the remaining guys in his platoon didn't exactly relax. Watching their colleague's head bounce down the stairs didn't have the calming effect I was hoping for.

Our ultimate goal for changing the outfitting experience had been to turn the clothing locker into a safe haven, not simply for measurement purposes, but because none of us working there wanted to contribute to the harsh treatment that was (in the 1970s) central to recruit training. We had all experienced it, hated it, hadn't bought into the notion that we "needed to be broken before we could be shaped into men," and wanted to see all vestiges of abuse abandoned.

We also knew we couldn't change the whole boot camp experience by ourselves. Nevertheless, we figured we could at least create a refuge where individuals were treated respectfully. We could stand at the border between the clothing locker and the rest of the base and do our best to maintain a professional and respectful atmosphere within our own domain.

Sadly, I didn't know how to be a border guard. Just ask that poor recruit. I'd have to learn to operate within both domains before I had any hope of succeeding in either. So, for the next year, I learned how to survive in the world as it existed. But day-by-day, I also learned ways to create the world I wanted.

For instance, I learned to give the boot-pusher a dollar. I'd suggest that he leave his platoon in our care and go get a cup of coffee at the club. "Don't worry," I'd enthuse, "we'll give you a call when we're through." Removing the primary source of terror went a long way toward helping the young men relax. We could finally do a proper job of outfitting them.

When it came to the rest of my job, I learned that no matter how poorly I was treated when given an assignment or command, I could pass it down the chain of command in a respectful and involving way. When it came to insults and threats, I didn't have to pay it forward. Over time, I discovered dozens of methods that allowed me to be an effective border guard.

Most of us assume the role of border guard more often than we think. As parents, we refuse to embrace some of our own parents' bad habits. That's good news for our kids. We do the same at work. We reject a company's long history of excessive control. Or perhaps we refuse to use guilt or threats to motivate.

But doing so isn't easy. Border guards frequently question their efforts. Can they really make a difference if they're not the CEO? The truth is, border guards make change possible. Organizations don't change one morning when twelve-hundred people awake and—*voilà*—simultaneously start acting differently. Changes typically take place in small groups, led by leaders who (whether they realize it or not) play the role of border guard. In fact, that's how the Coast Guard's boot camp was eventually transformed into an organization that now leads the country in human performance technology. Border guards made it happen.

I heartily applaud parents and leaders alike who have a clear vision of what they believe their culture can become—despite their current unhealthy circumstances—have the courage to fight for it, and have the savvy to make it happen. I congratulate them for having the pluck to stand at the border between their hopeful haven and the harmful world around them and boldly proclaim, "Not on my watch!"

IN SEARCH OF
TRESUS CAPAX

//

"Foolishness is more than being stupid, that deadly
combination of arrogance and ignorance."

PAUL DAVID TRIPP

When Mother woke me by poking me with a rolled up newspaper and pointing to the minus tide reported on the front page, I knew what she had in mind. Mom was after clams. Everyone in our family loved native clams fried in butter, and since you could dig them up for free, the tasty mollusks always fit our budget. The only problem was you couldn't find clams unless the bay was out farther than normal, so you had to wait for a minus tide.

As I sat down for breakfast a few minutes later, Mom plopped an empty gunnysack on my lap, silently signaling that she wasn't interested in two-inch native clams after all; she wanted their massive cousins—*Tresus capax*, or horse clams. These four-pound monsters, chopped and seasoned properly, made a tasty clam chowder.

"No!" I exclaimed in protest. "I can't catch horse clams; they're too fast for me."

"Don't worry," Mom explained. "I'm sending your brother with you."

Just getting to the clams turned out to be a real chore. Bill and I had to take a hike up and over a steep hill that stood between our residence and Chuckanut Bay—home of the horse clams. After an hour of trudging through brambles, nettles, and briars, we stumbled down the final slope of the hill bordering the bay, removed the burrs from our socks, and headed to the far end of the tide flat.

As we drew closer to our quarry, Bill let me in on the trick for capturing horse clams. "It's easy," he explained as we walked across the spongy tide flat. "You just look for the secret sign of a horse clam."

"Look for the secret sign!" I shouted. "I tried that with snipe hunting and that didn't work out so well for me."

"Shhhh!" Bill shushed me as he crept along, lowering himself even closer to the wet sand. "Do you see that mark over there about the size of a dime?" he whispered as he pointed to no place in particular. I glanced in the direction he pointed, positive that I would find nothing. But unbelievably, just off to his left was a small indentation.

"So?" I asked.

"When the tide goes out," Bill explained, "a horse clam burrows deep into the sand and then sticks its neck up a couple of feet until the tip just touches the surface. That tip makes the dime-sized mark we're looking at. It's a secret sign. Shove your hand into the wet sand just below the mark and squeeze tight. If you're fast enough, you'll grab the clam's neck and it won't be able to escape. Then, hold on and I'll dig down to the clam."

"*You* grab the slimy old neck," I responded, "and *I'll* dig out the clam." With that, Bill thrust his hand into the wet sand and pulled up a horse clam neck. Dang—it really worked! A couple of minutes of frantic digging later and we dropped a clam about the size of a large russet potato into our waiting gunnysack.

"I told you so," Bill enthused.

"I guess that'll teach him for sticking his neck out!" I exclaimed, marveling at my ten-year-old wit. Bill, who normally would rather take a blow to the head than admit I had said something clever, actually smiled.

A couple more tries, and we perfected the neck-grabbing technique. First, I'd grab and Bill would dig, then we'd swap jobs. An hour later, our gunnysack was half full of chowder makings, and we were ready to go home. Sadly, there was one more challenge we had to face. The hill. It had been hard enough hiking the mound without hauling a sack weighed down with mollusks.

"Let's take the shortcut," Bill suggested. My heart stopped. "Are you crazy? If a train comes, it'll kill us for sure." The shortcut he spoke of was a long, dark train tunnel we hadn't taken on the way to the bay, because we were fresh-legged, toting an empty sack, and in no mood to die. Now, exhausted from digging clams and hefting a heavy bag, my brother figured the tunnel offered benefits that far outweighed the risks.

"Don't worry, trains hardly ever come down this track," Bill argued. "We'll get through the tunnel lickety-split, and then it's a flat trail all the way home."

"But if a train does come, it'll squish us like a bug. I'm not going in there," I announced.

"Then *you* haul the bag up the hill," Bill countered.

Bolstered by my brother's refined sense of invulnerability, I followed him to the entrance, and we started into the darkness. The thought of being squished terrified me.

After Bill and I had lugged the bag about halfway through the tunnel, we suddenly heard the sound of a train. It made the hairs on the back of my neck stand up. We were at least five minutes away from the end of the tunnel, and it sounded as if the train was soon to be upon us. My brother and I ran for our lives. Dumbed down with terror, Bill sprinted toward the light at the end of the tunnel—failing to let go of the gunnysack full of horse clams.

It's hard to describe the sound of a train that's sharing a tunnel with you. As the screeching locomotive drew near, I checked my ears to see if they were bleeding. When the engine was only a few yards away, Bill pulled me down to the narrow strip of ground between the tracks and the jagged wall where we both lay as the iron horse roared by—sucking the air with it and pulling me closer to its wheels. Sensing my peril, Bill reached out with his right arm and pinned me to the ground as the train tugged at my body.

Five minutes after the train hurled passed us, Bill and I staggered out of the far side of the tunnel, clams still in tow. Then, in an act of stupidity seldom matched by anything smarter than a bowling ball, we bragged to each other about how everything had worked out to our advantage. Weren't we the clever ones! We took on the tunnel, we saved the long walk, and we emerged the victors.

Then, as Bill hoisted the gunnysack onto his right shoulder he bragged about our ability to trick horse clams. "Dumb clams," he shouted. "They stick their necks out and get caught every time."

"Only a clam could be that stupid," I chimed in.

Of course, the minute we walked into that tunnel we stuck our necks out every bit as far as those clams had. To make matters worse, we dressed up our stupid choice as a successful venture and then bragged about it.

Fortunately, this type of mistake can be avoided. Simply call dumb luck what it is—dumb luck. For instance, you disable a safety device at work in order to meet a deadline, and you succeed without getting hurt. Or you fail to use your safety gear when riding on a four-wheeler, and you have fun without getting hurt. Now comes your test. Don't make matters worse by treating your dangerous choice like a wise act. Instead, admit your mistake, and vow to never take that kind of excessive risk again. You may not save face by admitting to your errors, but you may save your life.

THE CAPTAIN'S FIREPLACE

"Eminence without merit earns
deference without esteem."

NICOLAS CHAMFORT

"**C**aptain Newton wants to speak to you," said the administrative assistant on the other end of the phone. *The captain?* I thought to myself. *Why would the Big Kahuna be calling* me, *a lowly ensign?* I would soon find out.

"This is Captain Newton speaking," uttered the firm voice now on the phone. "You know that large dumpster that sits in front of the supply building?"

"Yes, sir," I responded. "I think it's a Dempsey version, if I'm not mistaken."

"Whatever," the captain continued. "I've noticed the past few days that it's been filled with scrap wood. If nobody else wants it, I was wondering if it would be okay if I fished out a few pieces for my fireplace. That is, if nobody else wants it."

"I'll check with the appropriate people ASAP and see how to make it happen," I eagerly responded, taking pride in the fact that I had employed the military expressions "ASAP" and "make it happen" in the same breath. Next, I dialed the warrant officer in charge of supply and passed on the captain's request for the scrap wood—taking care to include the captain's proviso, "if nobody else wants it." The supply officer said he'd take care of it and get back to me.

Two hours later, it wasn't the supply officer who got back to me; it was the captain's wife. She thanked me profusely and repeatedly for the lovely wood for her fireplace. I graciously accepted her words of appreciation and then headed out to learn why the captain's wife was so incredibly grateful for a few scraps of castoff wood.

Before I could track down the supply officer, I overheard the following conversation at the water cooler: "You won't believe the old man. He calls us and demands that we cut up beautiful new boards for his fireplace. We go out to his house, measure the fireplace, cut expensive oak to fit it, band the wood, and deliver it— and all of this just so he can burn it!" Soon the base was abuzz over the captain's fireplace.

To find out how the original request had become so twisted, I talked to each of the men involved. Each had dutifully passed on the request to the person below him, while making slight changes in the wording. This was similar to the "telephone" game we played as kids. You whisper a silly phrase in someone's ear, that person whispers the same to the next person in line, distorting it slightly, and so on, until the original expression, "Mrs. Whipple has a pimple," comes out the other end as, "Whip the purple carburetor."

In this version of the "telephone" game, the chief warrant officer explained that he had called the chief petty officer and told him that the "old man" wanted the wood in the dumpster. Note the term had switched from "captain" to "old man," and from what I thought was a tentative request, "If nobody else wants it," to a mandate.

The next person explained that he had told his direct report that the old man wanted *new* wood for his fireplace. He figured they'd better not use scraps filled with nails and jagged edges and run afoul of the captain. The next in line thought he ought to measure the fireplace so the new wood would fit. Plus, you couldn't ask a captain to pick it up; he'd have to deliver it.

It wasn't long before a disgruntled team of Coast Guard enlisted men were cutting, measuring, banding, and delivering new oak to be burned in the captain's fireplace.

Unlike the "telephone" game in which the original expression follows a random path, the captain's request followed a sad and predictable one. The original request was altered to fit the story people were carrying in their heads about the captain—and all other senior leaders who ever abused their authority.

Rumors always follow this route. In order for tall tales to be shared, they must be *plausible*. If you suggest that a person everyone respects did something ghastly, typically the first person hearing the story stops, checks the facts, and otherwise refuses to besmirch the good name of someone he or she likes. The rumor never gets off the ground. In the case of the captain's fireplace, if one person had thought, *The captain wouldn't want us to cut up expensive lumber, let me go check,* the problem would have been averted.

For an unflattering story to be told and then retold and twisted into something as bad as the wanton abuse of government property, the listener must have it in his or her head that the bizarre actions contained in the story are just the kind of thing the person in question would do. The next person has to believe the same. But it gets worse. In this instance, the story that was passed down the chain of command was not about this particular captain at all (he was actually quite pleasant and thoughtful), but about everyone's image of a *typical* captain, and as such was infused with the characteristics of every abusive leader who came before him.

Captain Newton suffered from a prejudice just as pernicious as if it had been based on his race or creed. He was "one of them"—a senior leader, and we all know how they behave. They abuse their authority, jerk people around, and get what they want. Tainted by this mental set, and despite the fact that he was cut from a very different cloth, Captain Newton's innocent request was eventually twisted into a ludicrous demand.

None of us is immune to this phenomenon. Given the highly human proclivity to please the boss, coupled with the willingness to think the worst of others, leaders need to ensure that over-zealous subordinates don't reframe their suggestions into rigid and foolish orders. We would be wise to track our ideas as they flow through the organization. When a pile of worthless scrap wood turns into an expensive bundle of oak, this is not a feel-good moment. It's a bad sign.

As bizarre requests come our way, and they will, we have a responsibility to get to the root of the matter rather than simply pass on the absurd demand. We need to confront what appear to be senseless ideas and ridiculous requests from the get-go.

Start with your strongest leadership tool. Assume that others are rational—most people are most of the time, so they are probably unaware of any wacky misinterpretations. Search for the facts. Refuse to implement misguided ideas or commands until you've tracked down the original request and informed people about the potential consequences.

Otherwise, you'll be recreating your own version of "The Captain's Fireplace," and there are far better ways to warm your toes.

A SPITTER'S LAMENT

"We must believe in free will—we have no other choice."

ISAAC BASHEVIS SINGER

Since the dawn of humanity, philosophers, scholars, and puppeteers alike have been asking the same penetrating questions: "Do we have free will? Do we actually make choices on our own, or do powerful forces outside our control—or even our awareness—determine our behavior?"

Having no particular opinion on the matter myself, I skated through life unfettered by concerns about free will until the day my wife and I bought our first home. Along with a two-car garage and built-in dishwasher, our home came equipped with, of all things, a test of my free will. The test was cleverly disguised as a redwood deck, but, make no mistake, it was a free-will test, and I couldn't escape it.

Here's how the test worked. The first time I walked out onto our second-story deck to take in the exquisite view of Mount Timpanogos, I leaned over the railing, looked down on our new lawn, and spit. What?!

Before my saliva hit the ground, my wife pronounced me a filthy beast, and my two grade-school daughters squealed in disgust. But their reaction did little good. No matter how they reacted, every time I leaned against the deck's rail from that moment on, it pushed my spit button. It was creepy. I couldn't *not* spit. When it came to that deck, I had no free will whatsoever. I was little more than a puppet jerked into sudden action at the mere sight of the open space below me.

Eventually, I figured out what was going on. As a child raised around the docks of Puget Sound, like all of my boyhood friends, I spit every time I looked over the edge of any raised platform. It's what boys did when they peered off a dock.

In an effort to reprogram my spit reflex, I tried personal pep talks. I'd approach my deck and think, *Don't spit, don't spit! You can do it! You're bigger than the railing. You're better than the railing!* But then I'd get distracted—*Oh, a pretty butterfly!* I'd lean against the rail, and—patoohee—I might as well have been a cowpoke leaning over a spittoon. "Dad spit three times," my daughters reported to my wife when she returned home.

I mention this problem of reflexively jumping into inappropriate actions not because I want to enter the free-will debate, but because it's highly relevant to something I do care about—changing one's behavior.

Here's how the two topics relate. Many of our daily actions contain precious little free will, because they're so tightly scripted— like a stage play in which the characters know their lines and deliver them the same way, over and over again, without thinking. As Shakespeare once wrote, "All the world's a stage and . . . if a fellow gets near the edge, he'll spit every time." Okay, maybe not those *exact* words, but the world is indeed a stage and we play out simple and routine interactions by using the same scripts, tone, and nonverbal actions so frequently they often become rote. When pressed, not only can we play our part on the stage, we can play everyone else's part—so predictable is the script.

The good news is that these patterned responses free up our brains to fret about other things. The bad news is once we start into a script, it's hard to change what we do and say. We follow the script much like a familiar path—actually, more like a steel railway.

Let me share an example that doesn't involve saliva. One evening, my wife asked me to request extra packets of catsup when I placed an order at a hamburger joint. I entered the queue, waited my turn, and then the clerk started into the fast-food counter script. "May I help you?"

"Why, yes," I replied, and off we went. I didn't merely know what I was going to say, I also knew what the clerk was going to say. He was going to ask me if I wanted fries and a drink and when I said yes, he was going to ask, "Large?"

Of course, once I switched into autopilot, I flew through the interaction without much thought and, you guessed it, I didn't ask for extra catsup. I was never going to ask for the catsup, because the standard fast-food script had already been programmed into my brain. I started into the script, and once I had, I slipped into autopilot, coasted along, stopped making decisions, and did not ask for catsup.

It's important to realize that much of what we do—for better or worse—is so scripted that if we want to change either our own or others' behaviors, verbal persuasion will be nearly useless. We can't offer up a simple suggestion and expect others to immediately comply. Others may want to comply, but once they start down their programmed path, well, they won't be thinking about your advice. They won't be thinking about much of anything. So, what's a pre-programmed person to do?

One solution lies *not* in lecturing or chiding others, but in reminding them in nonverbal ways. This is only one of several tactics, but it can be so effective that it deserves attention. For example, when I finally tired of being ridiculed by my daughters for spitting off the deck, I put up a sign. Nothing fancy—not even words, just a simple line drawing of a spitting head with a line through it. The silly thing worked. I'd walk up to my redwood railing, see the sign, and catch myself before it was too late. Ergo, no more ridicule from my daughters.

This method of providing visual cues to prompt preferred behaviors has been used effectively in businesses for decades. For example, a hospital administrator tires of exhorting staff members to choose inexpensive but less comfortable plastic gloves over the ten-times-more-costly rubber ones. After failing to see changes in glove usage, he finally puts up a poster near the glove boxes with the prices of each option written in large letters. The use of the expensive gloves drops 80 percent. Staff members simply needed a visual reminder to keep them from falling into their routine.

When my business partners and I first designed and delivered interpersonal skills training, many of our graduates claimed they were having trouble remembering to use their newly acquired skills. To mitigate their knee-jerk and ineffective reactions, they put up posters that demonstrated their new verbal path. This visual cue helped many of them start down a healthier trail to problem solving. Now we provide posters as a routine part of the change process.

So the next time someone does something obnoxious, propelled by years of repeated actions that have solidified into a rigid script, replace your desire to lecture them with a simple visual reminder. Either that, or I have a couple of daughters who would be happy to follow them around and ridicule their every false step.

They have years of practice.

THE POWER OF PRAISE

///

"I love criticism just so long as it's unqualified praise."

NOEL COWARD

"**C**all on me!" I quietly implored as I used my left arm to hold my right arm high above my desk. Miss McCloud, my first-grade teacher (and the most wonderful woman to ever walk the earth), had just asked the class to identify the color of the flower in her hand. I waved my arm wildly, because I was confident in my answer. To be honest, I saw myself as a bit of a color savant. Plus, I really wanted Miss McCloud to admire me for knowing the correct answer so I could bask in the glow of her approving smile. Did I mention she was the most wonderful woman to ever walk the earth?

At that time in my academic career, I had been in school long enough to have figured out the three axioms of education: (1) questions have right and wrong answers, and it's good to give the right answer; (2) it's even more satisfying to give the right answer after someone else has given the wrong answer; and (3) it's pure bliss to give the right answer after *everyone* else has given the wrong answer. Then Miss McCloud really piled on the praise.

As the years passed, the axioms didn't change much, but the nature of the questions did. By the time I was in college, the average query was far too complicated to be satisfied with a simple answer. I still raised my hand every chance I got in hopes of gaining attention, but rare was the day when others gave a flat-out wrong answer that I could easily correct in order to earn the professor's special approval.

So I had to learn a new skill. I had to learn how to spot flaws in others' arguments. Sure, my classmates would offer answers that were mostly correct (or at least correct in principle), but if I applied myself to the task, I could always find a flaw, point it out, and grab the spotlight.

When I moved on to grad school, I discovered that finding flaws in what others had to say wasn't merely a fun hobby, it was academia's prime directive. My classmates and I would sit in our Colosseum-shaped classrooms, listen to each other's comments, eagerly spot a mistake, and then, in gladiator fashion swoop in and strike down the egregious logical lapse or factual *faux pas*. We were nit picky, we were brutal, and we loved it.

Later, when I became a team leader, I used my growing talent for detecting mistakes by practicing what is known as "management-by-exception." I wouldn't say much to my direct reports when they were doing well—that would be disruptive. However, if they took a misstep, I'd speak up immediately so the problem wouldn't escalate.

Raising children was no different. My eyes were drawn to mistakes far more often than they were to successes. Nobody walks by two children playing quietly and praises them for playing quietly. It's inconceivable. If kids are playing quietly, you don't even *see* them, let alone praise them.

Once, when I was working in Brazil, my "spot-the-error" routine was challenged. Dale Carnegie, in his classic *How to Win Friends and Influence People,* suggested that in order to be a decent human being, I ought to look feverishly for things done well and then offer up hearty approbation and lavish praise—not just once in a while but all the time.

If this wasn't radical enough, Carnegie challenged me to praise a total stranger just to see what it was like. Of course, to follow his advice, I would have look up the word "approbation" and spot something praiseworthy. If anything should be clear by now, it was that I hadn't been trained to see "things gone right." For several days I looked for a praiseworthy accomplishment, but to no avail.

Then I finally struck gold. I was riding a bus through the streets of a small town near Rio de Janeiro. Inside my head Dale Carnegie was screaming, "Look for something good!" It was really annoying. Suddenly, the young man taking money for the bus fare caught my eye. He had a dreadful job. He sold bus tickets by winding his way through a crowded, speeding bus. People crabbed at him, the driver ridiculed him, chickens pecked him, and then there was the ghastly smell of a crowd of passengers who believed that bathing was for sissies. In spite of all this, the young man was the picture of professionalism.

I told him just that. I pointed out how well and quickly he made change. I mentioned that I admired his ability to keep his balance and remain polite and pleasant. And I meant it.

Bingo. I had done it. I had followed Carnegie's admonition about approbation. Now what? First came a pause. The guy was thinking about what I had just said. Finally, the young fellow smiled widely and gave me a big hug. Tears were running down his cheeks.

The bus employee introduced himself as Carlo Pereira. He explained that he had dropped out of school at age fifteen and worked as a ticket taker to help support his mother. I was the first person who had ever praised him, despite the fact that every single day for three years he had tried to do his best. Carlo then introduced me to everyone on the bus as his "American friend," and from that day forward wouldn't accept my money if I happened to board his vehicle.

Carlo's devotion only grew. As I was walking down the street one day, he had the driver pull over and pick me up. Then Carlo told the driver to change routes so he could deliver me to the door of my next appointment—which, as you might guess, didn't go down well with the other passengers. They were about to be transported blocks away from where they were originally hoping to go and were now threatening to cause Carlo bodily harm. Carlo didn't care. I was the only customer he was concerned about. I was the only person who had ever complimented him.

Naturally, I was stunned by Carlo's reaction to the heartfelt but simple praise I had expressed. But later I made sense of Carlo's response. I learned that in annual corporate surveys, the number-one complaint of employees is always the same. Their leaders don't recognize them for doing a good job.

Since most bosses go through the spot-the-error educational system I went through and see their own leaders routinely model management-by-exception, they too focus on problems, not success. In fact, generous praise isn't even a small part of most leaders' influence repertoire. Employees hate this lopsided treatment. They do their best work and look around to see if anyone notices, but nobody does. It turns out *everyone* is Carlo. Everyone is waiting for a heartfelt compliment.

And now for the punch line. *You* can be the stranger on the bus. Maybe you already are. But if you aren't, or aren't as often as you'd like to be, now's your chance. Supplement your talent for spotting problems with the ability to see things going right. Then break years of tradition, and say something. Remember, be hearty in your approbation and lavish in your praise. Not because you want a free ride for the rest of your life, but because Carlo is doing a wonderful job every single day—and he deserves to hear it from you.

WHEN THE GOING GETS TOUGH

//

"It's time for us to turn to each other, not on each other."

JESSE JACKSON

In September of 1970, I found myself in Yorktown, Virginia. Along with 320 other recent college grads, I would be shaped into the Coast Guard's latest version of an officer and—according to the brochure—a gentleman. To be perfectly frank, I was scared to death about being *shaped* into anything. The word on the street was that this shaping would be done by terrifically muscled, sadistic instructors who would do their best to humiliate, degrade, and otherwise turn me into a whimpering shell of a human being.

Or so went the rumor. But then again, these were the laid-back, hippie-centered 70s. Surely our training would be all hearts and rainbows. Sure enough, that first evening when I met one of the officers who would be training us, Lt. Larry Thompson, I knew we were in for a good time. Larry invited me, along with a couple of other officer candidates, to his dining table, where we ate fried chicken and told jokes. Then Larry pulled out a photo of his wife and two tiny tots. I still remember how cute his kids were. They had button noses.

That evening, as several of us trainees sat in the common area watching TV, Manny Epstein, an officer candidate from Brooklyn, enthusiastically chatted about how much fun our experience was going to be. Obviously, as Manny argued, the rumors we had heard had been wrong. We weren't going to be insulted, threatened, and abused—this was the Coast Guard, not the Marines!

The next morning as we meandered out to a place that looked very much like a parking lot stained with blood, I was surprised to see that my friend Larry was coming at me at a dead run. I was so startled by his rapid approach that I actually looked over my shoulder to see if someone was on fire. What else could fill him with such a sense of urgency? Only, as Larry drew closer, I noticed that he looked as if he was feeling more anger, maybe even hatred, than urgency.

It turns out that Lieutenant Thompson, the proud father of two button-nosed tots, wasn't about to save a life; he was about to crush mine. Not knowing what to do, I gave him my best imitation of a salute—half *McHale's Navy*, half *Hogan's Heroes*. Disgusted by my pathetic attempt, Lieutenant Thompson forced me and my cohorts to do push-ups until we wished we were dead.

This abuse continued for a few hours until we finally took a break—the other thirty members of my platoon and I waited for a chance to receive "free government inoculations." Ah, the perks just never stopped coming.

As I stood in line wondering if I had made a poor choice in signing up with this lot of nautical sadists, I heard, "Pssst!" The guy standing behind me was trying to get my attention. Should I turn around and talk to him? Heck no. It was probably a trap. If I turned around, surely one of Satan's henchmen would have shouted, "Mr. Patterson! Don't you know that turning your head while standing in line for typhoid shots is a violation of the Geneva Convention and is punishable by death?"

So I didn't move a muscle. A minute passed, and I heard another "Pssst!" Then another. And another. Eventually, I noticed that the hissing had a bit of a Brooklyn accent. It had to be Manny Epstein, the guy from the evening before—the guy who had talked about how *fun* the training was going to be—and he wanted to say something.

"Psst!" I couldn't ignore Manny any longer, so I threw caution to the wind and craned my head in his direction. Manny looked horrible. He was a good forty pounds overweight, and the torture we had just endured had almost done him in. His face was ashen gray, and his body quivered like the Pillsbury Doughboy in a wind tunnel.

When I turned around, Manny muttered four words I'll never forget. With a twinkle in his eye and a Brooklyn accent you could cut with a knife, Manny said, "Da jam-ba-ree is ova." I laughed so hard it cost me fifty pushups.

Sadly, Manny was right. Our dreams of passing peaceful evenings listening to officers tell tales of fun-filled times on tropic isles were utterly crushed. No more jamborees for us. For us, it would be marching in scorching heat, lying on our backs doing imitations of a dying cockroach, and being yelled at until we wanted to fall into a crack in the earth.

I eventually graduated from officer training, served three years in the Coast Guard, exited into the civilian world, and never looked back. That is, until decades later, I found my training yearbook tucked away in the corner of my office. I opened it, and there staring back at me was a photo of my platoon, Alpha-1. The picture had been taken during the heat of that horrible first day, and we looked dreadful.

As my eyes worked their way across the photo they eventually settled on the fellow in the bottom right-hand corner, Manny Epstein. He didn't merely look dreadful, he looked defeated. As I stared at the telling image, I wanted to go back to 1971 and attend OCS again; only this time, I wanted to get it right.

The first time we went through training, we had been told that if we dropped out (or were thrown out) of OCS, we'd be demoted to an enlisted rank and sent to Vietnam to die. With this threat hanging over our heads, we turned into a group of selfish louts. When the going got tough, we got selfish. When I say "we," I mean "I." I watched Manny Epstein struggle and did nothing to help him. I knew all kinds of tricks for helping him square away his personal grooming as well as his quarters, but I never shared any. And when Epstein inevitably was whisked off in the middle of the night, nobody spoke of him again.

And so, Mr. Epstein, I apologize. You were right about the jamboree being over. We were about to face hard times, and that should have been a call for us to pull together, not turn on each other. I know I needed your help (Manny was a wiz at piloting), and I suspect you needed mine. But I didn't know I was allowed to help. I didn't know I should help. I was young and frightened.

Fortunately, over the ensuing decades, most of us have come to realize that we need to collaborate with our colleagues if we expect our companies to succeed. We need to act like teammates, not combatants. This should be true of all work groups. Everyone deserves to work with colleagues who pull for them, support them, and pitch in as needed. If that's not your current reality, it should at least be your aspiration. When the chips are down, we should find a way to help one another. Because if we don't find a way . . .

Da jam-ba-ree is ova.

FINDING JOY AT WORK

//

"The supreme accomplishment is to blur
the line between work and play."

ARNOLD J. TOYNBEE

The TV shows I watched as a boy typically began with a father
coming home from work, dressed in a suit and tie, carrying a
briefcase, and whistling a happy tune. Based on dear old Dad's
smile, you'd guess he worked at Disneyland.

Of course, you never knew for sure. The moment Sitcom-Dad
stepped over the threshold, that would be the end of any work references. No writer dared bring down the jolly mood with sordid
details about the nature of work itself. Consequently, the oft-re-
peated message of the 50s was as vague as it was odd. People went
to work in order to engage in mysterious activities that left them
whistling peppy tunes at the end of the day.

This image, of course, was in no way representative of the people I knew. My neighbors didn't own a briefcase between the lot
of them, and they most certainly didn't wear suits. They wore thick
aprons and gloves to keep the gunk, slime, and muck off their
clothes. Not once did I see anyone whistle on his or her way home
from work.

Given the circumstances on our side of the tracks, adults complained endlessly about the backbreaking and mind-numbing
nature of their jobs, along with the stupidity and pettiness of their
bosses. It was hard to know what they despised more—the work

they did, or the supervisors who made them do it. It's what they talked about. It's what they told jokes about. It's what they wrote songs about.

Imagine my surprise twenty years later when I found myself humming a tune as I walked out the door—*on my way to* work. I loved what I did. I neither wore a suit nor carried a briefcase, but somehow I had found a way to extract pleasure from my job. And yes, I even whistled once in a while. But why? It couldn't have been the work itself. Half of my colleagues didn't like their jobs one tiny bit.

Two decades passed before I met Rich Sheridan, a renowned entrepreneur and organizational philosopher who knows a great deal about job satisfaction. Rich once started a software development company with the belief that creating software (some of which involved actual cartoon figures and cool sound effects) would be fun. How could you not have fun while making the corporate version of video games?

But then Rich learned that customers, no matter how yippy-skippy the product, often changed their minds in the middle of the development cycle. This led to tension-filled meetings with lots of finger-pointing and gnashing of teeth. Plus, the code writers who worked with Rich soon became specialists—making it impossible for any of them to leave work early or, heaven forbid, take a vacation.

For Rich and his development team, what had started as a romp down candy cane lane was now a torturous grind through the valley of unfulfilled expectations. Where had he gone wrong? How could he turn his company into a place that left him with a tune on his lips?

Rich discovered the answer. He made an extensive study of joy and then infused his company with it. Best of all, his book—entitled *Joy, Inc.*—details how to create an intentionally joyful culture. Now, I'm not going to cover what Rich discusses in his book, but I will suggest the following. The *one* idea you should take away from Rich—or, for that matter, all job-satisfaction gurus—is that the sitcoms of the 50s were right. You *can* indeed love your work. You can whistle as you walk through the door each night. But you have to want it, believe it's possible, and then work for it.

I myself have experienced a bit of a work-related transformation as of late. For years I enjoyed a job that consisted of traveling the world, consulting, writing, and designing training. Then one day, I found I'd had my fill of travel. Just like that, I was done. So I decided to devote my time to writing. Surely, this would bring me joy. After all, I loved writing.

I was wrong. Writing can be lonely. Soon, I didn't care all that much for my job. It involved far too much isolation, mumbling, pacing, mumbling *and* pacing, as well as self-ridicule. Unlike my childhood neighbors, I wasn't breathing sawdust or gutting salmon all day long. But like them, I was unhappy at work. So I prepared myself for retirement.

Luckily, I recalled my visit with Mr. Sheridan and the case he made for creating joy at work. I felt inspired to find ways to infuse my own job with joy. It involved restructuring my daily tasks and working with someone with whom I could collaborate, while occasionally reenacting bits from old Three Stooges movies. I once again look forward to work.

How one goes about finding pleasure in his or her job varies. I don't want to underestimate how much effort and risk it might take to negotiate for more interesting work, restructure your job, or possibly even switch companies altogether. But if you don't like your work, you ought to do something about it.

For detailed advice, Mr. Sheridan can teach you about creating a company filled with joy. Daniel Gilbert can alert you to what it takes to be happy in general. Mihály Csikszentmihályi can teach you the elements required to enjoy any specific task at work. There's plenty of help out there—once you decide to seek it.

My point is far more modest. We should *expect* to find joy at work, and if it's missing, we need to go out and seek it. After years of hearing about lousy jobs and reading statistics that suggest most employees don't like their work, many of us have come to conclude that work equals dissatisfaction. This can be so deeply embedded into our psyches that it keeps us from asking for more.

But we should ask for more. We spend more time at work than just about anywhere else. It ought to bring us a full spectrum of positive emotions—pride, fulfillment, a sense of belonging, and joy, to name a few. This doesn't mean that in the ideal workplace employees routinely chase each other with Silly String. Nevertheless, celebrating a customer victory or excitedly sharing a success story should be common. Feeling fulfilled should be common. Laughter should be common.

So as we think about our jobs, our default position should be that work—organized correctly—is pleasurable. If it isn't, we need to make changes. Once this expectation is firmly set in our minds, we'll start taking steps to create joy rather than to create elaborate coping mechanisms. From what I've experienced, joy is worth the search.

Of course, Silly String doesn't hurt.

HOLIDAY LESSONS

THE GREAT VALENTINE'S DAY DEBACLE

//

"Trust yourself. You know more than you think."

BENJAMIN SPOCK
(PEDIATRICIAN AND CHILDCARE EXPERT)

Dr. Spock never met me.

One Saturday evening, I realized that I had only an hour left to buy my wife, Louise, a Valentine's Day gift. I was a grad student at the time, and Louise was working on a project across campus. So I quickly loaded our six- and four-year-old daughters into the backseat of our Volkswagen bug, strapped our eight-month-old son into a plastic baby carrier, and headed off to the nearest shopping center I could find.

With Becca, Christine, and a Raggedy Ann doll connected to me in a daisy chain of handholds and Taylor swinging gently in the plastic carrier clutched in my other hand, we found ourselves scurrying through a shopping center unlike any place I'd ever been before—mainly because it didn't have "Mart" or "O-rama" in the title. This posh facility obviously catered to the wealthy of Silicone Valley and not to poor grad students like me. It was positively brimming with beautifully attired, perfectly coiffed people.

Since I had been cleaning my outdoor grill when I bolted to buy my wife a gift, I looked more like the Maytag repairman than a

Palo Alto shopper. My kids looked as if they had just been plucked from a sandpile in our back court, which they had. As we nervously scuttled through the place, other shoppers' genial smiles turned into looks of disapproval as they scrutinized our scruffy clothes, our home-cut hair, and our barely opposable thumbs.

Eventually, the four of us found our way to the home center of a snobbish department store, where they had on display the very present my wife had hinted she wanted—a variable-speed blender, complete with pulse control. A perky clerk was soon wrapping up the bright red appliance I had chosen in honor of Valentine's Day.

As the clock continued to run, the girls and I scampered out into the shopping center in search of an affordable card.

"Daddy," Christine uttered, "don't you think—"

"Shush," I replied as we hurried past one high-end store after another. "I need to find your mother a card. One that says, 'I love you' on the front and not $6.00 on the back."

"I know," Christine continued, "but—"

"No buts about it. If I don't find a card, I'm in trouble."

Taking a more direct approach, three-year-old Rebecca asked, "Where's baby Taylor?"

It was like being hit by a bucket of ice water. There, in the hand that had once carried my son, was a package containing a variable-speed blender—complete with pulse control. Where was baby Taylor?

"He's back in that big store," Christine offered as she pointed to the far end of the shopping center. Egads! I had left my son in a blender display.

"The place is closed," explained a fellow walking by as I rushed up to the department store. "It's Saturday night."

"But I left my so . . . ," I cut myself off midword. "But I left something inside."

"You'll have to go around back to the employee entrance," the kindly fellow explained.

The girls and I scurried along a terribly long wall while employees coming off shift disgorged from a lone door at the far end of the building. The people walking our way were all talking about some idiot who . . . (well, you can guess). Then, as they saw me hustling along with my two remaining kids in hand, they quickly concluded that I was the fool they had been bad-mouthing.

They wanted me in jail. I just tried my best not to look like a convicted felon.

Eventually, my daughters and I found ourselves inside the building, standing next to a knot of folks who were cooing pleasantly while my son, still in his plastic carrier, smiled back politely. I searched for the proper words.

"Has anyone found a baby? It seems I've lost one." No, that would land me in jail.

"Funny thing, I came with three kids, and now I have only two. Go figure." Equally lame.

Eventually, I blurted out, "You've found my son! Thank you. Thank you. Thank you."

Pointing out that they had *found*, rather than that I had *lost*, my son appeared to take the edge off the pack of angry store clerks. After staring at me indignantly for a half minute, the lady in charge saccharinely asked, "Do you think you can get him home without losing him?"

"I brought my Raggedy Ann," Christine remarked as she held up her well-worn doll, "and I didn't lose her."

"Yes, dear and I'm very proud of you," I muttered back. Looking the authority figure directly in the eye, I mumbled, "So, we'll just be heading on home now." With this lame pronouncement fresh off my lips, I snatched up Taylor and retreated while the folks behind me stared daggers into the back of my head.

"Do we tell Mommy the secret?" Christine asked as we walked to the car.

"No!" I blurted. "We mustn't tell Mommy that I bought her a blender. It would spoil the surprise, and we don't want to do that!"

"No, I mean how you left Taylor in the store and then got locked out?" I was doomed. There was no way I was going to be able to keep the two girls from tattling on me. And sure enough, when we pulled up in front of our apartment, the little snitches bolted from the car to tell Mom the exciting news.

"You left Taylor in the store and then got locked out?" Louise asked incredulously as I presented her the brightly wrapped gift.

"Yes. Can you believe it?" I exclaimed in a futile attempt to deflect the blame. "Those bozos locked me out! And they claim to have good customer service." Nothing.

So I gilded the lily. "But you haven't had a chance to see the lovely gift I bought you. I was so focused on expressing my deep love for you with this truly special household item—complete with pulse control—that I just lost focus, you know, for a second."

"You didn't lose focus," Louise accused, "you lost Taylor!"

"I didn't lose my Raggedy Ann," Christine offered.

And so passed the Great Valentine's Day Debacle of 1977, which I now give to you freely and openly. Maybe you miss a birthday. Or perhaps a loved one becomes angry at you for not flossing your kids' teeth adequately or keeping them from getting hurt on a seesaw. You can say, "True, I messed up. But at least I'm not as irresponsible as that dimwit who left his baby in the middle of a blender display!"

This is my gift to you.

A MOTHER'S DAY MESSAGE

//

"A punishment to some, to some a
gift, and to many, a favor."

LUCIUS ANNAEUS SENICA

I was looking for lead pennies in the change tray behind the candy counter at Grandpa's store when Chuck O'Hanlon hurled his massive bulk through the front door. Chuck's body didn't allow him to enter a room quietly. His misshapen feet forced him to lean forward at a tilt that precariously propelled him across the floor until his cane eventually brought him to a rumbling halt.

"A pack of Luckies!" Chuck shouted to my grandfather, who was now standing behind the counter. The two men exchanged friendly banter as Grandpa rang up twenty-three cents on the cash register and handed Chuck two cents in change. I watched as Chuck gingerly leaned on the counter, awkwardly rifled through his right front pocket, pulled out a wooden match, dragged it across the cash register, and then put the flame to one of the cigarettes he had just purchased.

I liked Chuck. He was always friendly, and even though I was only a kid, he treated me like a real person. I felt sorry for him, though. His feet were horribly turned in, and you could tell that it took a great deal of effort, accompanied by a lot of pain, just for him to get around. I had no idea what had happened to him, but I knew that it wasn't something I should ask him directly.

But we did talk. Whenever I ran into Chuck at my grandpa's store or around the neighborhood, we discussed baseball. We were both fans. On this particular day, as Chuck puffed on his cigarette, we chatted about Dizzy Dean and what a terrific announcer he was.

"He hit the ball nine miles," I shouted in my best Dizzy Dean voice.

"Four and a half up and four and a half down!" Chuck finished. Then we laughed. It was pleasant having a real conversation with an adult, even though I was only seven.

"What happened to Chuck?" I asked my mom over the canned tamales we had for dinner that evening. "Why can't he walk like everyone else?"

"I'm afraid it was his mother's fault," Mom responded.

"Melba!" my father inserted, unhappy with what he thought was an attack on Chuck's mother. Dad had no patience with speaking ill of others.

"Well, it's true!" Mom said. "Chuck was born with his feet turned in. The doctor prescribed corrective shoes that would eventually fix the problem. But every time she put on the shoes, little Chucky would cry. The shoes hurt—they had to in order to do their job.

"Chuck's mom couldn't bear to see her son suffer, so one day she simply stopped making him wear the shoes. Now Chuck is a grown man, and he'll never walk normally. It's his mom's fault, because she gave in to his complaints."

This was my first encounter with the concept of "tough love." I could see Mom's point, but couldn't totally grasp the idea. It had too many facets for my young mind.

Now, insisting that someone *else*, such as Chuck's mother, do the hard thing in the short run in order to provide a benefit over the long run—why, that was easy. Under similar circumstances, we'd insist that little Chucky wear his corrective shoes. It's easy to make such a claim when you've never actually held him in your arms, stared into his eyes, and listened to his whimpering.

To her credit, Mom demanded that she herself administer that same brand of tough love whenever called for. It wasn't long until I discovered this firsthand.

As I hurried home from school one day, I ran into "Redheaded Rodney," the eight-year-old boy who lived just up the hill on the way to our house. Rodney asked me to come and play with him. I explained that I had to go straight home from school, or I'd get in trouble. Rodney didn't care about our family's silly rules, and since he was bigger than I was, he told me he'd beat me up if I didn't stay and play.

An hour and a half later, when I finally arrived home, Mom was standing on the porch with her arms folded. This wasn't going to be pleasant.

"Go cut a switch," Mom insisted as she handed me a knife. This was new. I had to cut the switch that Mom would use to punish me, and it wasn't even my fault. What was the world coming to? After a careful and rather slow search, I returned with a switch small enough to not hurt much but not so small as to anger my mother further. She immediately put me across her knees.

"But Mom," I cried. "Rodney made me play with him. I wanted to come home on time—honest!" Swat! Mom wasn't taking excuses. She also wasn't taking any satisfaction. Out of the corner of my eye, I could see a tear slowly running down her left cheek. Mother never used a switch on me again—although as the years unfolded, she did find plenty of other ways to discipline me. I also was never late coming home from school again.

Decades later, as I drove my now eighty-year-old mother to the market, I happened to catch a glimpse of what looked like the adult version of "Redheaded Rodney" in the rearview mirror. The memory of that switch immediately came to mind.

"Hey!" I accused. "How come when I was just a little kid and I came home late from school because 'Redheaded Rodney' made me stay and play with him, you punished me? It wasn't my fault!"

"I hated doing that," Mom explained.

"So why did you do it?" I asked.

She responded, "Five days a week you walked home from school all by yourself, a full mile and a half down a road that was surrounded with all kinds of temptations and dangers. I knew if I let you stop and play with friends, skip rocks on the pond, chase waterskippers, and the like, you'd never get home on time, and who knows what would have happened to you.

"Plus, you had a very inventive mind," Mom continued. "If I accepted your explanation that a bully forced you to stay and play, you'd have ten more reasons for being late the next day and twenty more the day after that. I despised spanking you that day. If I had done what I wanted, I would have taken you into my arms. But I did what I thought was best for you."

Mom understood tough love. As I recall that incident, it's the tear running down Mom's cheek I remember the most. I don't know if spanking me was the right thing to do. I'm certainly not advocating corporal punishment, nor did I rely on it as a parent. But I do know Mother was doing what she thought was right, even though it hurt her.

So Mom, for Mother's Day this year, let me say this—thanks for adoring me when I did the right thing. And equally important, thanks for being tough when I didn't.

A SOLDIER'S MEMORIAL

///

"Heroes are people who rise to the
occasion and slip quietly away."

TOM BROKAW

W hen I was a young boy and our extended family gathered, it
was common for the adults to congregate in the dining room
and play cards while we kids romped around our backyard. But
not always. Sometimes my Uncle Vic would slip away from the
adults and sit out on the porch with the kids.

It was Vic who showed me how to press two fingers to my lower
lip to create a wolf whistle. It was Uncle Vic who taught me how
to tie a cat's cradle, how to spin a button on a string, how to make
a coin disappear, and dozens of other childhood tricks and games.

I often wondered why my uncle so readily broke away from the
rest of the adults just to spend time with a kid. One day, shortly
after he passed away, I asked my mother why Uncle Vic was as
likely to spend time with me as he was to mingle with his peers.
Vic's actions were particularly curious given that his wife, Aunt
Mickey, was such a vibrant, vocal personality. I couldn't imagine
how she ever ended up with such a quiet man.

"Don't you know what happened to your uncle?" my mother
asked. "When my sister first met Vic, he was outgoing, oozed confidence, and looked the part of a movie star. Why, when he and
Mickey walked into a restaurant, the crowd hushed and stared at
them. It was as if celebrities had entered the room."

"And then what happened?" I asked.

"World War II," she explained. "It happened to all of us—only more so to Vic. You see," Mom reluctantly continued, "your uncle joined the army and was eventually sent to the Philippines, where he was put in charge of a platoon. It was the job of Sergeant Victor Veloni and his team to clear the remote islands."

"Clear them of what?" I asked.

"Enemy soldiers who stayed behind to wreak havoc with the American troops and Philippine civilians. Surely you've heard about them? You know, the soldiers who perched in trees waiting for a chance to cause mischief for anyone who came into view. Vic and his team would land on an island and then do whatever was required to remove the tree-dwelling snipers."

"What's that supposed to mean?" I asked. I could tell that Mom didn't want to talk about the details.

"Vic and his team would police the island until someone would shoot at them, and then they'd deal with the sniper."

"They walked around until someone shot at them!" I exclaimed.

"Mostly," Mom replied. "It was the best way to draw the enemy into the open."

I could hardly imagine tramping around a steamy, tropical island in full military gear while waiting for a bullet to pierce my helmet. It's beyond comprehension.

"Wasn't that dangerous?" I asked.

"Dangerous?" Mom said, somewhat incredulously. "Vic ended up losing most of the men in his platoon and half of the replacements. One by one, he lost his dear friends and comrades as they fell prey to sniper fire. Our prayers were answered when Vic came home alive. But, given the loss of his comrades, he never forgave himself for doing so."

"And that's what changed him?" I asked.

"When the war ended and your uncle returned to Seattle, I hardly knew him," Mom continued. "He was the same handsome man who had gone off to war, but the vibrant, fun-loving Vic that used to live behind that chiseled face was no longer there. The horror of watching his friends die, the tension of waiting for the next bullet, the self-imposed guilt for not taking one of his own—it killed the Vic we knew and left behind the man you grew up with. Not everyone who survived the war actually survived the war. Vic went off to battle, but somebody else came home."

I had no idea about any of this. I was just glad my uncle had spent time with me. I simply wanted to know why he so willingly left his friends to play with a nephew.

Not long ago, teenagers from our neighborhood Boy Scout troop posted a flag in our front yard to honor the Fourth of July. My thoughts turned to the scores of people—like Vic—who have sacrificed in so many different ways so that we can enjoy our many freedoms.

As the Scouts unfurled the flag, I thought of a different group of boys I had taken to a military cemetery. As these young men and I gathered on a peaceful hillside just outside San Francisco, we stood by the graves of decorated soldiers and read aloud the detailed stories of the selfless acts that had earned each fallen soldier both his medal and his grave.

With each news broadcast about the military, my thoughts turn not only to these young people and others who have fallen in the field, but also to those who have returned home—many injured, all affected, and some, like my Uncle Vic, transformed into a completely different person.

When TV news commentators talk of the number of wounded and killed in certain battles, or when statistics pop up on the screen to summarize what's happening overseas, I don't see the numbers. I don't think of the statistics. Instead, I see an image of my Uncle Vic.

It's not the image you might imagine. It's not a crowd gathered to pay homage to his sacrifice. I don't see a general draping a medal around his neck. Nor is it a band trumpeting his glory. It's far more humble and more important than any of that. It's the image of a little boy holding a cat's cradle string and sitting on the lap of a true American hero.

MEMOIRS OF A PROFESSIONAL TRICK-OR-TREATER

"There is a child in every one of us who is still a trick-or-treater looking for a brightly lit front porch."

ROBERT BRAULT

'll start this shamefully self-promoting story with a brazen assertion. I firmly believe that I was the best candy grabber in the history of Halloween.

"Pshaw!" you say? Well, here's the evidence.

As I walked home with my best friend, Rick Eherenfieldt, one crisp October afternoon in 1955, he asked, "Do you want to go trick-or-treating with me?"

What a hayseed! What a rube! Didn't he know anything about the finer art of extracting candy from strangers? Going door-to-door with friends is unthinkable. When you travel with friends, you talk, and talking slows you down.

Trick-or-treat rule number one: During the precious few hours of the one night of the year when candy is free for the asking, don't slow down for anything. Every moment lost could cost you a candy bar—which, by the way, just happens to be your only reason

for going door-to-door in the first place. It's all about the chocolate.

"One Halloween evening as I sprinted down the street," I
replied to Rick, "I came upon a house that was on fire, and I didn't
break stride. Do you think I'm going to slow down just to talk
with a friend? I don't think so."

Here's another time-related hint. Today's kids tote plastic pumpkins and other such sissy containers for holding their
goodies. I carried, and I'm not making this up, a burlap bag that
originally contained fifty pounds of potatoes. I chose this beast,
because I didn't have time to be swapping out cutesy bags midway
through the evening.

Of course, choosing a ratty-looking gunnysack caused me some
grief. By the end of the evening, a potato sack jammed with candy
weighed just about as much as I did. Equally bad, a lot of people
were offended by it.

"Look at that disgusting sack!" one lady chided as I held out the
bag large enough to schlep a yak. But I didn't care. I wasn't trying
to impress old ladies with scruples. This was Halloween. I was on
a chocolate quest.

Rule number two: Run from door to door. When you only have
a five-hour window to get free candy, you run. You don't walk. You
don't jog. You don't skip, saunter, swagger, strut, or ramble. You
don't even trot. You run at full speed, and you run the entire five
hours. Am I making myself clear here? This is free chocolate we're
talking about!

Now, to be perfectly honest, not everybody took advantage
of the full five-hour running period allotted annually. I couldn't
imagine what they were thinking. I was always the first and last
kid on the street. Every year, my Halloween adventure started
with, "It's not time yet, you little twit! I'm still doing the lunch
dishes!" and ended with, "You woke me out of a dead sleep!"

Rule number three: Put the trick back in trick-or-treat. The
candy companies of the mid-50s didn't produce the shameful
miniature bars they now make in such abundance. So when some-

one gave you a candy bar back in my day—and I firmly believe this qualified them for sainthood—you got a full-sized candy bar. This didn't happen very often, but when it did, you scored big.

So, here was the trick. I'd carry three masks. I didn't normally wear a mask, because it would limit my vision and slow me down. But if someone gave me, say, a full-size Hershey bar, I'd hit a couple of other neighbors' doors, put on a mask, and then return to the place that was giving out the mother lode. I would repeat this stunt with a different mask until they caught on to me. "Say, kid, haven't you been here before?" I once scored five Almond Joys from the same house.

Rule number four: Beware of baked goods. I was raised at a time when a handful of Betty Crocker wannabes shunned store-bought treats and made cupcakes frosted with an inch of gooey chocolate icing. They'd beam with pride when they opened their front door. "Here you go, Sonny," they'd say as they held out a tray full of baked concoctions while giving the stink eye to my burlap bag. What was I supposed to do with a cupcake? Eating it was out of the question. That violated rule number five: *Never* eat on the job.

One year, I made the grievous error of letting a grandmother drop a cupcake into the center of my bag. I swear the thing had its own gravitational field. It sucked every decent piece of candy into its icing atmosphere until, by the end of the evening, it had grown to the size of a medicine ball. I learned to take cupcakes gingerly in my hand, smile politely, walk to the next house, and then use them to mulch the flowerbeds.

Before actually writing this Halloween advice, I had never shared this material with my own children. As helpful as it might be to a budding trick-or-treater to learn these priceless tips, I feared that they would make me look bad. You know—desperate, greedy, and weird.

This hesitance to share the less sugarcoated side of my past raises an interesting issue. When you primarily share your accomplishments with loved ones and acquaintances—as the majority of us do—and fail to share your embarrassing moments, weaknesses, and vulnerabilities, you're less interesting. You're less human. And worst of all, you don't make all that good of a friend. Nobody likes hanging out with a hundred-and-fifty-pound ambulant résumé.

The same could be said for your relationships at work. I'm pretty confident in assuming that almost everyone has an unflattering story about their own holiday habits—things they'd prefer to keep locked away rather than share with their coworkers. But the truth is, sharing nothing but accomplishments instead of a debacle or two creates more distance than unity. In contrast, sharing oddities, fears, and *faux pas* produces the very glue that binds people together.

So, when the next Halloween season rolls around, dare to be vulnerable. Consider donning a new costume. Not one shielded by masks of sobriety, perfection, and accomplishments. Rather, let your friends and coworkers get a glimpse into the more interesting you—the geek you, the childlike you, the oddball you.

For example, did you ever have a costume malfunction and accidentally moon your neighbor? Did you soap someone's windows only to learn that it was the principal's house? Did you aggressively knock doors on Halloween night until someone finally shouted, "Hey, kid, it's time to haul your potato sack home!"

Knowing stuff like that binds families and work teams together. And that can be a real treat.

A CHRISTMAS GIFT

//

"The greatest gift is a portion of thyself."

RALPH WALDO EMERSON

I t was December of 1984, and my wife, children, and I were
eagerly buying presents for a teenage boy we had never met as
part of a Sub-for-Santa adventure we were engaged in, along with
four other families—with each family buying presents for one
child from within the same household. It would be our third year
attempting to help a needy family, and we approached the task
with a mix of emotions. Could we truly help someone? Would we
be a blessing in their lives? Or would we disappoint them? We had
experienced both positive and negative results in the past.

Two days later we nervously scooped up the presents we had
purchased, packed up food and clothing, and piled into our cars.
Excited about what lay ahead, we drove through a chilling drizzle
to a small house that displayed the address we'd been given.

"It looks tiny," said my oldest daughter as five cars chock-full of
parents and children pulled up to the house. Gingerly, we carried
the boxes to the front porch. Not knowing what else to do, we
huddled together in the freezing rain and started to sing carols.
Eventually, the father took pity on us, stepped out into the rain,
and invited us to come in.

Minutes later, as twenty-five of us stood cheek to jowl, the
father began to speak. He explained that he had undergone back
surgery earlier that year and hadn't yet been able to return to work.

It hadn't been an easy choice, but he'd decided that if they were going to have any presents for the children, he'd have to call on one of the local agencies. He thanked us profusely for answering the request for aid.

"Now, in exchange for your presents," he continued, "I offer you one of my own—in the form of a story. A few years ago, when we had only two children, we were again facing a meager Christmas. We bought my oldest son, who was eight at the time, and his sister, who was four, two presents each. One was a pair of socks, the other a toy. My son had asked for a basketball, and from the size and shape of his two packages under the tree, there was no doubt which one contained the ball."

The boy, who was now a gawky teenager, stood shyly in the hallway, nodding in agreement. "One evening, two days before Christmas, I came home with an announcement. A family had moved in nearby, and since they didn't have two pennies to rub together, they wouldn't be having a Christmas. They had a boy and girl the same ages as ours, and I was thinking that maybe we could share Christmas with them.

"'We could give each of them one of our two presents,' my wife suggested as our children looked on in dismay. After staring at his two presents for what seemed like an hour, my son finally walked over, picked up the package containing the basketball, and said, 'I'll share this one.' Each of us then grabbed one of our two presents, put it in a box, and carried it down to our new neighbors, who seemed very grateful."

As we listened to this father's story, I glanced over at my own children. Their eyes were fixed on him, brimming with tears as they thought of how these people had sacrificed so dearly.

"Later that day," the father continued, "I received a phone call from our local church leader. He explained that there were a few families in our church group who didn't have any money for Christmas. Catching wind of the problem, a group of generous parishioners had put together several boxes of presents and food. Since we owned a station wagon with plenty of room, he asked if we would be so kind as to drive to the church on Christmas Eve, load up the wagon, and make the various deliveries. 'Besides,' my church leader explained, 'your two young ones will get a kick out of playing Santa.'

"I immediately agreed to lend a hand, but I knew that by doing so, we would have a problem. I explained to my family what I had committed to do and then shared with them the challenge. We had spent all of our money on Christmas, and our station wagon was almost out of gas. We'd have to find a way to raise some cash to put fuel in the tank.

"'We could collect soda pop bottles,' my daughter suggested. This was something she had seen her older brother do in order to earn money. If you retrieved a pop bottle by the side of the road and took it to a local grocery store, they'd give you two cents. So we bundled up against the wind and snow, and all Christmas Eve day, we hunted for bottles. Just before we were due to make the deliveries, we cashed in the bottles, put a couple gallons of gas into our old wagon, and drove over to the church.

"As our church leader loaded box after box filled with beauti- fully wrapped presents into our run-down vehicle, my son and daughter looked on in wonder. They sniffed the air with a look of longing as he loaded a carton containing freshly baked pies and a ham with all the trimmings. They squished over to the edge of their seat as the boxes were stacked one upon the other, until our wagon was filled to bursting. My son looked on in envy as he spot- ted a package the exact shape and size as the one that had con- tained the basketball he had given away.

"Our church leader then handed me an envelope containing a list of the various names and addresses of the people we were to visit, and he thanked us for helping with the deliveries. As he drove off, I opened the envelope to see the size of the task in front of us. The small piece of paper I found inside the envelope con- tained but one name and address. It was ours."

As the humble man finished his story, those of us who had come to help his family were either openly crying or doing a poor job of holding back tears. I was completely humbled as I envisioned this sweet couple and their two children bracing against the wind and searching for bottles, doing their very best to help the needy.

What made the story all the more wonderful was that he had done his best to make the church leader and the other members of his congregation out to be the heroes—look how nice they had been to his family, he had explained—just as we were being nice to them this year.

It had never occurred to him that as thoughtful as his church friends had been to his family, our Sub-for-Santa gang looked on him and his children with a genuine sense of amazement. They were the ones who shared their Christmas. They were the ones who had trudged through frozen fields on a quest to serve the needy as others drank hot cocoa by the fireplace. They were the true heroes, and they didn't even know it.

My family and I cherish our sweet experience with this remarkable and selfless family as our favorite holiday gift. It is a present that will live with us forever.

STUMBLING ON CHRISTMAS

//

"We didn't starve, but we didn't eat chicken unless
we were sick, or the chicken was."

BERNARD MALAMUD

The winter of 1956 was a hard time for the Patterson family. Our woes began when Dad came home from work at the lumber mill in such horrible pain he could scarcely drag himself through the front door. He had tripped at work and severely injured his back.

After gutting it out for a few days, Dad put himself in the care of a surgeon who chose to fuse Dad's spine. Two weeks later, when Dad returned home to heal (and not work), the money we would live on for the next few months would have to come from whatever Mom could earn by baking and selling wedding cakes and petit fours.

The neighbors soon caught wind of our plight, and hardly a day passed without someone stopping by with a slab of venison or a basket of wild asparagus. Occasionally, a friend would drop off fresh fruit or even a salmon. Walter Kaiser, the retired boatswain's mate who lived across the street, brought by a huge bag of unshelled peanuts he'd won playing bingo at the Veterans of Foreign Wars.

As fall drifted into winter and Dad was still laid up, my thoughts turned to Christmas. Without money for presents, I wondered if the peanuts would be our only gift that year. What I really wanted was a ten-inch reflective telescope. I'd found a picture of a fantastic looking one in a catalog, but I knew it didn't fit our budget. So I put in a request for an inexpensive plastic spyglass.

Mom could tell I wasn't adjusting well to our newfound poverty. She did her best to remain cheerful, despite the fact that our financial crisis was exacting a toll on her. Between caring for Father, raising two boys, and making baked goods, Mother scarcely slept, and yet she was our rock.

One evening, Mom found me crying in my room. My weekly allowance had been long abandoned, and I had suddenly realized I had no money to buy presents for my relatives. Now what would I do? Mom comforted me while she searched for a solution. "Let's see," she fussed. "You don't have any money. I don't have any money . . . ." Then it came to her in a flash. "Walter's peanuts!" she shouted with glee. "Walter's peanuts!"

Mother then explained that she would teach me how to make peanut brittle for Christmas. A box of brittle would make a delicious present, and we already had all of the ingredients. For several evenings I donned an apron, stood on a stool, and labored over a pot of bubbling sugar. Soon I had a present for everyone on my list, and my Christmas cheer seemed to appear in greater supply with each batch I completed.

But my holiday mood didn't last. There was no sign of a spyglass anywhere, and I was just sure my tenth Christmas was going to be the worst one ever. Once again, it was Mother who came to the rescue. As I sat at the kitchen table mooning over the Sears catalog toys I wouldn't be getting, Mom gently tapped me on the shoulder. I turned around, and there she stood with her arm outstretched and an ax clutched in her hand.

"It's time for you to go get our Christmas tree," Mother said with a smile. I couldn't believe it. The ax was being passed on to me! Drawing myself out of my funk, I carefully took the ax from Mom's hand, hiked into the snow-covered forest behind our house, and chopped down a spruce tree.

An hour later, as I huffed, puffed, and hauled the newly cut tree to our home, I ran into Walter. "That's a shabby-looking thing," the former navy man barked as he bit down on his pipe. He was right. The well-shaped trees were too far away for me to haul them all the way back to our home, so I had settled on a scruffy-looking thing that was nearby.

"I have just the ticket," Walter offered as he disappeared behind his house. A few minutes later he returned with his solution to our shabby tree—a hand drill and several drill bits. "Every place there's a gap in the tree, drill a hole in the trunk," Walter snapped. "I'll tell you which drill size and where to drill." After I finished boring the holes, Walter handed me a stack of limbs he'd cut from a pine tree nearby and said, "They're not a perfect match, but they're close enough for government work."

Uncertain but hopeful, I began to insert pine branches into the holes I had drilled in the spruce tree. Then, with Walter's help, I cut the newly affixed appendages to the right length and trimmed a little here and a little there until the tree looked surprisingly full—motley, but full.

Christmas day finally arrived, and all I could think about were the presents I had made. How would my family react? I didn't have to wait long to get an answer. Soon my relatives were sampling the peanut brittle I had made.

"It's wonderful!" my Aunt Mickey exclaimed.

"And you made it all by yourself!" Grandpa added.

"Why, it's far better than anything store-bought," offered my Uncle Vic.

"And just look at the tree!" my father said proudly. Then he paused for effect and asked, "Did you know that Kerry is responsible for that tree?"

"I heard you cut it down yourself," Grandpa stated.

And so, in a flurry of compliments and joyful affirmations, our 1956 came to an end. By mid-January, Dad had returned to work at the mill and life was back to normal.

I hadn't thought much about that particular seàson until a few days ago. My attention turned to several friends who were financially strapped, and I considered the challenges they might face as they tried to bring joy to the holidays.

I don't know what it will be like for others; however, I do know this. In 1956, the year of our poverty, I didn't get a spyglass. We simply didn't have enough money. But you know what? It didn't really matter. I still found Christmas. I found it in Mom's irrepressible spirit and endless ingenuity. Dad constantly praised me for growing into what he called "a little man." That was his gift. My family complimented the brittle and the tree I cobbled together with the enthusiasm generally afforded a returning hero.

This year, several of my family members are taking their lead from 1956. Many are making gifts rather than buying them. My nine-year-old granddaughter, Rachel, has sewn a bunting for her newborn sister. I suspect her gift will get most of the "ooohs" and "ahhhs" at the Patterson gathering this year. I suspect that it'll be Rachel's favorite gift as well.

We're also taking special care to spend as much time as we can together. Our love of time shared together will be the biggest part of any memory we'll create. And when we gather for the holidays, I plan on reading this story to my grandchildren. I'll give other gifts. I'll share other things. But they're only things. This story, taken from memory and recorded with love, will be my favorite gift.

So there you have it—1956 was the year of our poverty. It was the year my father tripped . . . but somehow *I* stumbled onto Christmas.

I SHALL CHERISH
IT FOREVER

//

"Christmas is not a time nor a season, but a state of mind."

CALVIN COOLIDGE

One December morning, as my five-year-old son Taylor and I bought gifts for his two older sisters, he turned to me and asked, "What was your bestest Christmas present ever?"

I have thought about that question over the years since. Despite the fact that as a child I had pored over the toy section of the Sears catalog, much like a monk musing over a sacred manuscript, my favorite gift never made it into Mr. Sears's marvelous book. More curious still, it sat in a box, unopened for nearly fifty years.

To appreciate this magical gift, you have to know a little about how the human mind works. I like to think of it as thousands of tiny shelves that sit in long rows inside our head. On these shelves sit millions of even tinier boxes. And inside these boxes you find memories.

Some of the boxes remain unopened, and the thoughts left inside evaporate like dry ice on a summer day. Other memories remain active and vital, because we often pull those boxes off the shelves, open them, and relive their experiences.

Of course, every time we open a memory box we change the contents. When we visit a memory, we add a little here and snip a little there. With each new peek, we make subtle alterations. One day, all that's left is the memory of a memory—little more than a faint and distorted copy. The original is gone forever.

But not always. Every once in a while, the most amazing thing happens. A mysterious force knocks a box off one of our memory shelves, and a container that has sat untouched and tightly sealed for years bursts open. When it does, you relive a precious moment—unchanged and straight from your childhood.

That's what happened to me one morning a few years ago. I was preparing for a Christmas visit from my granddaughter. As I tried to make the house safe for a curious child, I spotted a small, shiny object on the floor just under our living room couch. As I drew closer I could see that it was a dime.

"We can't have that lying around," I mumbled to myself as I dropped to my hands and knees. At that very moment, a song I had learned in the first grade started playing on the radio. "Christmas is coming. The goose is getting fat." The image of the shiny dime coupled with the melody of a long-forgotten childhood song pushed an untouched package off my memory shelf.

Whoosh!

As the lid from this tiny box popped open and the contents tumbled out, I was suddenly six years old. The dime I had been staring at under the couch magically transformed into a dime lying under my grandfather's candy counter.

When I was a boy, my grandpa owned a corner grocery store. Every day, on the way home from elementary school, I stopped by to see him. He always wore a pale-green apron that looked clean, stiff, and official.

I loved my granddad as much as I loved anyone or anything. And Grandpa loved me in return. He was proud of everything I did. When I earned a gold star at school, he acted as if I had invented penicillin. Even when I didn't do very well, he smiled warmly and told me not to worry.

Sometimes Grandpa would use me as a prop. On rainy days, I'd stop by the store and he would go through the same routine.

Grandpa would be chatting with a grownup customer, and as soon as I'd walk up next to him, he'd mention how miserable the weather was. Then he'd look out at the drizzle and say, "You know, I wish the sun would come out, not so much for myself but for my grandson." Then he'd pat me on the head and explain, "I've seen the sun before, but my grandson never has!" Everyone would laugh.

On this day—that is, the day that fell down from my memory shelf—I was on my hands and knees doing what little boys do when they're at their grandfather's grocery store next to the candy counter; I was looking for coins. Sometimes grownups dropped a penny, and if you were lucky, you'd find one and end up with a tasty treat. Only this time, I spotted a shiny new dime. Ten whole cents!

I can still remember what I bought—one licorice whip, one red-hot jawbreaker, two sour cherries, one raspberry vine, and ten Whoppers—Whoppers were two for a penny. Grandpa smiled so wide as I scampered out of his store you would have thought that he was the one with the pocketful of candy.

The next day, when school came to an end, I ran out the back door, raced down the hill, burst into Grandpa's store, and dropped to my knees in anticipation of having a repeat experience. I crawled around, looked, sniffed, probed, and hunted until miraculously, I found another dime! This time I bought my older brother an Oh Henry! candy bar and myself five pieces of penny candy.

And so it went. Every day I'd drop to my hands and knees, find a dime, and marvel at my good luck. Sometimes I'd only spend five cents, and the next day I'd buy a fifteen-cent kite. All through that spring and well into the summer I bought Fudgsicles on hot days, kites on windy days, and candy bars when I was thinking of my brother. And every single day, Grandpa would smile wide as I ran from the store with my treasures in hand.

This was the box that fell from my memory shelf when I knelt to pick up a dime the day my granddaughter was coming for Christmas. The entire rush of thought—complete with Whoppers, kites, and licorice whips—passed in a flash.

As I arose from my hands and knees nearly fifty years after finding that first dime, the adult inside me returned. *Why, Grandpa!* I thought to myself, *You put those dimes there, didn't you!* At age seventy-two, Grandpa had gingerly lowered himself to the floor and secretly hidden a dime in a different spot each morning.

I had a friend growing up who was given some of the most amazing gifts for Christmas. The year he turned sixteen his parents gave him an entire automobile. Not just a leather steering-wheel cover, or one of those scented cardboard pine trees you hang on the rearview mirror—but an entire car. If his five-year-old son were to ask him about his "bestest" Christmas present ever, I bet he would talk about that shiny red Chevy. But for me, my favorite gift was a memory that fell off a shelf and bathed me in the warm glow of my grandfather's love.

Sometimes when I'm feeling blue, I open that glorious box and look at the kites and penny candy and relive the joy. Sometimes the box falls down all by itself. When it does, I taste the sweet Fudgsicles, feel the tug of a kite, and imagine my grandfather on his hands and knees, hiding a dime for his beloved grandson. And even though my "bestest" present was never listed in any department store catalog, that extraordinary box—that memory box filled with Grandpa's love—is far more precious than anything shaped by human hands. And it is one I shall cherish forever.

AUDIO DOWNLOAD: Listen to Kerry tell his story, "I Shall Cherish It Forever"

To access an MP3 download of Kerry narrating this story, as well as other free resources from *The Gray Fedora*, visit **www.vitalsmarts.com/bookresources**.

THE SECRET'S OUT

//

"I'll tell you a secret. Old storytellers never
die. They disappear into their own story."

VERA NAZARIAN

A s a boy growing up in small-town America, I attended a church
where the speakers were selected from ordinary congregants.
The good news: We heard from all sorts of people. The bad news:
They often gave lousy speeches. Some so bad that by age twelve
my buddy Ron Gunn and I started timing speakers to see how
long it would take until more than half of the audience was no
longer paying attention. It generally took about four minutes.

Now, it's not as if we got up and left when we became bored.
That would have been rude. My friends and I escaped into the
blank spaces of the weekly church bulletin, where we played connect-the-dots, tic-tac-toe, and hangman. Adults viewed these
games as disrespectful, so to avoid their own boredom, they typically placed head in hand and elbow to knee (very Rodin-like) to
give the impression of paying attention without actually doing so.

One Sunday, Homer Jackson, a church official from Seattle, visited us small-town heathens to make sure we hadn't dropped a
commandment or two. He ended his inspection by preaching the
weekly sermon. As usual, Ron and I were prepared. During an
invocation that lasted about as long as it takes to read the Magna

Carta, we covered our weekly bulletins with a matrix of unconnected dots. We were tedium-ready.

Then Homer surprised everyone by giving a riveting speech. The effect was amazing. Not a single adult pulled a "Rodin," babies stopped crying, and Ron's great-grandpa (who hadn't been awake during church since the Hoover administration) opened his left eye and showed signs of brain activity. Most remarkable of all, Ron and I listened to everything Homer had to say.

After the meeting, the two of us discussed the reason the speech had been so effective and concluded that it was due to his delivery. Homer had been delightfully animated. There were points when he spoke at a near whisper, but then he would build to a loud, fast-paced crescendo, hit us with an ingenious punch line, cut back to a haunting mutter, and have us begging for more. Homer had been on fire!

Ron and I hoped the adult congregants in attendance had picked up on Homer's trick of speaking with a lot of energy—for future reference. It was, in our opinion, the key to capturing and maintaining an audience's attention.

A week passed, and the scheduled speaker was now Hyrum Yoakum—an ordinary local. As an insurance salesman, Hyrum knew a great deal about high-energy presentations, maybe too much. While waving his arms wildly and shouting barefaced insults, Hyrum combined actuarial tidbits and threats of eternal damnation into a sermon so frightening it snapped everyone to attention. For about three minutes. Then Hyrum's unrelenting harangue grew tiresome. Two minutes more of his ruthless railing, and it was Rodin and hangman all around.

"Just being energetic doesn't necessarily make for a good speech," Ron stated as we exited the building. "It worked for Homer, but not for Hyrum. Listening to him was like being attacked."

So we hadn't figured out the key to being a successful speaker. A snappy delivery, while perhaps important, wasn't enough to carry a sermon. It needed something more.

Several months passed (one connect-the-dots Sunday followed by another) until Martha, a congregant in her mid-seventies, stepped up to the podium. She spoke quietly—so quietly, that I immediately reached for a pen. But when Martha started to talk about how her great-grandmother had crossed the plains, we all sat up and listened.

Martha's great-grandmother, Annie Muldoon, started her trek from Ireland to the mountains of Idaho on a transatlantic boat. Each morning, she and her fellow passengers were forced to submit to an inspection to discover who had the strength to stand. Weakened by bad weather, Annie couldn't remain upright on her own, so two of her traveling companions secretly held her dwindling body between them. Had Annie fallen or sagged noticeably during any of the inspections, the captain would have thrown her overboard. Apparently, they hadn't purchased the "no drowning" upgrade.

For nearly an hour, Martha told Annie's story of traveling to New York and then crossing the wild-animal-infested plains. It was so fascinating, vibrant, and real that Ron and I never put a mark on the bulletin. Martha had a nice delivery—no denying it—but it was her story that kept our attention. Ron and I had finally uncovered the secret. If you want to capture and hold an audience's attention, tell a story.

Since those early days at church, I've watched hundreds of speakers at school, business conferences, and public events as they've tried to win over audiences. Nothing has changed. If speakers deal exclusively in abstractions and theories—no matter how clever, new, or loud they are—they soon fall flat. If speakers don't tell an engaging story with a smooth and varied delivery, they have only a few minutes until audience members pull a Rodin, chat with neighbors, fiddle with electronic devices, or play games with their grandfather on the back of a bulletin.

It's not as if this concept is new. For centuries, playwrights and novelists have made a living telling stories. Nowadays, even advertisers use them as their influence tool of choice. For instance, a TV commercial that is currently running shows a young man adjust his tie, pin on a boutonniere, and borrow his dad's car keys. Then he drives to the high school, defiantly parks in the principal's parking space, walks across a crowded dance floor, steals a kiss from the prom queen, and gets punched by the prom king. As the scene ends, the young man glances back and catches an approving smile from the queen. Then comes the tagline, "Courage. It's what defines us." This bit of Hollywood magic was ostensibly created to convince viewers to have courage. But in truth (in case you missed it), it was designed to sell a German car.

Imagine working for an ad agency and trying to convince a team of German engineers that the best way to sell their car isn't through showcasing the nifty gadgets they've been working on for decades and love like their own children. Instead, the agency proposes a commercial that shows a goofy teenager driving to the prom and stealing a kiss. The proposed ad will barely show the car and reveal none of its features. Not one.

So why would the ad win approval? When people view the prom story, they *feel* something. That feeling holds their attention, sticks to their brain, and eventually drives their behavior. Stories outperform conceptual discussions, lists, and charts every single time. Behavioral scientists study this phenomenon, advertisers use it, and—believe it or not—German engineers occasionally approve it. Parents and leaders have made the same discovery. Savvy ones add poignant stories to clarify the "why" behind any call for change. They highlight characters, tell their story, generate feelings, and eventually change behaviors.

So there you have it. During my own lifetime, stories have extended their domain from books, stages, and screens into corporate boardrooms, family kitchens, political gatherings, and (if I'm lucky) the sermons I listen to on Sundays. Sometimes the stories are written. Sometimes they're spoken. And sometimes they're told by a broken-down management consultant who, in the place of a traditional theoretical discussion, reaches back into his own life and dusts off a story or two.

He hopes you've enjoyed them.

ABOUT THE AUTHOR

Kerry Patterson resides in Provo, Utah, with Louise (his wife of more than forty years), there the two are holed up in their basement designing custom-fitted drool cups for their dotage. Close by live their four children, their spouses, and their combined fourteen children who can clear a restaurant in minutes from the horrific clatter of the silverware alone.

Down the hill from the Pattersons, you'll find one-hundred-and-thirty employees working skillfully and diligently in the offices of VitalSmarts, a training company Kerry cofounded with his partners Al, David, Joseph, and Ron who still put up with him, despite the occasional drool-cup reference.

Peppered throughout the United States, you'll run across a couple dozen executives Kerry consulted with to create lasting improvements in key performance indicators—which is not nearly as amusing as it sounds.

Six hundred miles to the northwest, you'll find Bellingham, Washington. It was here that Kerry grew up and was nearly dragged from a moving car, blown to pieces, burned up, and eaten by sharks—but somehow managed to escape in order to share stories about these fascinating places, wonderful people, and the lessons they teach us.

For more information, visit **crucialskills.com/grayfedora**.

WANT MORE? Download three bonus stories from Kerry Patterson

To access a PDF download of three stories that didn't make their way into *The Gray Fedora,* as well as other free resources, visit **www.vitalsmarts.com/bookresources**.

ABOUT VITALSMARTS

An innovator in corporate training and leadership development, VitalSmarts combines three decades of original research with fifty years of the best social science thinking to help organizations achieve new levels of performance. Specifically, we focus on human behavior—the underlying written and unwritten rules that shape what employees do every day and create the cultural operating system upon which an organization functions.

VitalSmarts' work within the halls of some of the world's top organizations has led us to identify four skill sets present in successful companies. When used in combination, these high-leverage skills create healthy corporate cultures that spur flawless execution and consistent innovation. These skill sets are taught in our award-winning training programs and *New York Times* bestselling books of the same titles: *Crucial Conversations*, *Crucial Accountability*, *Influencer*, and *Change Anything*.

VitalSmarts has trained more than one million people worldwide and helped more than three hundred of the Fortune 500 realize significant results using this proven method for driving rapid, sustainable, and measurable change in behaviors. VitalSmarts has been ranked by *Inc.* magazine as one of the fastest-growing companies in America for ten consecutive years.

www.vitalsmarts.com

ATTEND A **VITALSMARTS**
TRAINING COURSE

PERSONAL
Self-directed change
Successfully solve any individual
behavior challenge—at work or at home.

INTERPERSONAL
Open dialogue
Foster open dialogue around high-
stakes, emotional, or risky topics.

TEAM
Universal accountability
Enhance accountability, improve
performance, and ensure execution.

ORGANIZATIONAL
Influential leadership
Drive rapid and sustainable behavior
change for teams and even entire
organizations.

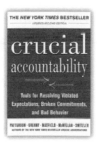